"*Did God Really Say?* engages the discussion of the doctrine of Scripture, offering keen and relevant insight into its current issues. The ideas presented are paramount to the church and will be of particular benefit to those seeking to defend the doctrine of Scripture."

—**Alistair Begg**, Senior Pastor, Parkside Church, Chagrin Falls, Ohio

"Current discussion about the nature of Scripture circles around a plethora of topics, each of them painfully complicated. Here a handful of scholars tackle seven of them—including the nature and development of the canon, the place of Warfield, God's relation to language, and the views of N. T. Wright. With firmness and fairness, not to say remarkable simplicity, these writers identify the fundamental issues and bring clarity to their joyful confessionalism."

—**D. A. Carson**, Research Professor of New Testament, Trinity Evangelical Divinity School, Deerfield, Illinois

"The appearance of this volume is most welcome. At a time of increasing doctrinal imprecision and indifference, with all-too-evident disastrous practical consequences for the life of the church and its mission, its authors uniformly address issues related to Scripture's nature, authority, sufficiency, and clarity in ways that are timely and beneficial. I commend it highly for a broad audience."

—**Richard B. Gaffin Jr.**, Professor Emeritus of Biblical and Systematic Theology, Westminster Seminary, Philadelphia

"In every generation the church has to rearticulate its confidence in Scripture. From our first parents in the garden to our Savior in the wilderness to the apostle's charge to Timothy, the issue has been the same: 'Did God really say?' How we answer that question will affect—for better or worse—the health of the church, our witness to the world, and the state of our souls. This book does not dodge the bullets or sound an uncertain note. Rather, it clearly and convincingly restates the historical and biblical account of Scripture's most basic claim to be God's Word written."

—**Liam Goligher**, Senior Minister, Tenth Presbyterian Church, Philadelphia

"The contributors who have given us this volume are committed not only to high academic integrity, but also to the highest view of Scripture. . . . They patiently and clearly set out the truths and principles that not only have upheld the Bible through the centuries but also have preserved the church in her devotion to Christ."

—**Mark G. Johnston**, Senior Pastor, Proclamation Presbyterian Church, Bryn Mawr, Pennsylvania

"The authors believe that the authority of God's Word is derived from the Word itself. They hold that the church doctrine of divine inspiration is a faithful summary of what the Bible teaches regarding its own inspiration. They are not content merely to articulate the doctrine; they call the church to follow its implications by bowing in the dust before the authority of God's inerrant Word."

—**David B. McWilliams**, Senior Minister, Covenant Presbyterian Church, Lakeland, Florida

"Dr. David Garner has wonderfully given us a volume that appropriately affirms, defends, and defines the reliability and sufficiency of God's Word, and at the same time equips the reader not only to profit from the Word of God but also to defend its priority and integrity. I invite you to savor every page in this book."

—**Harry Reeder**, Senior Pastor, Briarwood Presbyterian Church, Birmingham

"Just when the inspiration and inerrancy of Scripture seemed matters of agreement among conservative theologians, along comes a new day that calls everything into question again. . . . *Did God Really Say?* clears away the rubble of contemporary error and prejudice, making way for clear thinking and orthodox confession on an issue of vital importance. Nothing could be more crucial for our times, and we are in their debt."

—**Derek W. H. Thomas**, Minister of Preaching and Teaching, First Presbyterian Church, Columbia, South Carolina; Distinguished Visiting Professor of Systematic and Historical Theology, Reformed Theological Seminary

# DID GOD REALLY SAY?

*Affirming the Truthfulness and Trustworthiness of Scripture*

Edited by DAVID B. GARNER

P&R PUBLISHING

P.O. BOX 817 • PHILLIPSBURG • NEW JERSEY 08865-0817

Cover image: "Fall" from *The Holy Bible, conteyning the Old Testament and the New: newly translated out of the originall tongues; & with the former translations diligently compared and reuised by His Maiesties speciall comandement. Appointed to be read in churches* (Stewart, 1041). Courtesy of the Digital Image Archive, Pitts Theology Library, Candler School of Theology, Emory University.

Cover background texture © istockphoto.com / archives

Printed in the United States of America

**Library of Congress Cataloging-in-Publication Data**

Presbyterian Church in America. General Assembly (39th : 2011 : Virginia Beach, Va.)
 Did God really say? : affirming the truthfulness and trustworthiness of Scripture / David B. Garner, editor.
  p. cm.
 Includes bibliographical references (p.    ) and index.
 ISBN 978-1-59638-399-9 (pbk.)
 1. Bible--Evidences, authority, etc.--Congresses.  I. Garner, David B., 1965-
 II. Title.
 BS480.P69 2011
 220.1--dc23
                              2012001798

To my parents,
who love the Word of God

"I bow down toward your holy temple and give thanks to your name for your steadfast love and your faithfulness, for you have exalted above all things your name and your word." (Ps. 138:2)

# Contents

# Foreword

THE THEOLOGY of the twenty-first-century global church is being fashioned with tools forged in what has been termed a "hyper-hermeneutical age." Thus, theologians, pastors, and laity experience a whirling world of disparate meanings and divided commitments. Seminaries and congregations alike inhabit this world of garbled communication, which enters its greatest confusion when discussions turn to ultimate concerns, especially the nature of Holy Scripture.

Accordingly, we are no longer surprised that Protestant leaders, even if calling themselves evangelicals, project creaturely limitations onto the Scriptures. The theological and hermeneutical (interpretive) principles employed reflect the self-absorbed logic of postmodernity:

- If we cannot understand our contemporaries' views and commitments, how much less can we understand the ancient Scriptures?
- Since the Scriptures are human writings, don't they possess the limitations of all other human communications?
- Aren't these limitations exacerbated by the historical anomalies of time and space?
- Don't human cultural concerns and self-interests overshadow or even dominate whatever inescapable authorial intent the Scriptures may present?

- Even if the Scriptures are the Word of God, how can mere finite creatures, especially untutored laypeople, possibly apprehend the transcendent mind of God cloaked in such obscure texts?

The results of the convergence of such perspectives with modern higher critical methodology and postmodern individualistic relativity are clear. The Bible is a book no longer suitable for the laity. Instead, a higher class is required, namely, scholars who are the sole legitimate interpreters of Scripture. Some have gone further and claimed that the Bible is a book without any definite meaning, since everyone's interpretive view of Scripture has an equal claim to the truth. In reaction to this claim, others have asserted that the proper posture of a contemporary viable faith in the message of the Scriptures is retreat into a secret meeting of shared discourse among specialists that defines the meaning of Scripture for its readers.

How different all of this is from the bold call of the Reformation's *sola Scriptura* and its attendant doctrine of the inherent clarity of Scripture! The first chapter of the Westminster Confession of Faith, "Of the Holy Scripture," well summarizes this historical viewpoint: the Scriptures are necessary,[1] inspired,[2] authoritative,[3]

1. "It pleased the Lord, . . . for the better preserving and propagating of the truth, and for the more sure establishment and comfort of the church against the corruption of the flesh, and the malice of Satan and of the world, to commit the same wholly unto writing: which maketh the Holy Scripture to be most necessary; those former ways of God's revealing his will unto his people being now ceased" (WCF 1.1). "The whole counsel of God concerning all things necessary for his own glory, man's salvation, faith and life, is either expressly set down in Scripture, or by good and necessary consequence may be deduced from Scripture" (WCF 1.6).

2. "Under the name of Holy Scripture, or the Word of God written, are now contained all the books of the Old and New Testaments. . . . All which are given by inspiration of God to be the rule of faith and life" (WCF 1.2).

3. "The authority of the Holy Scripture, for which it ought to be believed, and obeyed, dependeth not upon the testimony of any man, or church; but wholly upon God (who is truth itself) the author thereof: and therefore it is to be received, because it is the Word of God" (WCF 1.4).

infallible,[4] perspicuous (clear),[5] translatable,[6] self-interpreting,[7] and the very voice of the Holy Spirit.[8] Indeed, the Scriptures as the Word of God not only are infallible ("infallible truth and divine authority thereof")[9] but also present an infallible hermeneutic ("the infallible rule of interpretation of Scripture is the Scripture itself").[10] The Spirit who indwells us to receive and understand God's Word is the same Spirit who inspired it. Thus, the Scriptures are truly clear in their central message— even to the laity:

> All things in Scripture are not alike plain in themselves, nor alike clear unto all: yet those things which are necessary to be known, believed, and observed for salvation, are so clearly propounded, and opened in some place of Scripture or other, that not only the learned, but the unlearned, in a due use of

4. "We may be moved and induced by the testimony of the church to an high and reverent esteem of the Holy Scripture . . . and the entire perfection thereof, are arguments whereby it doth abundantly evidence itself to be the Word of God: yet notwithstanding, our full persuasion and assurance of the infallible truth and divine authority thereof, is from the inward work of the Holy Spirit bearing witness by and with the Word in our hearts" (WCF 1.5).

5. "All things in Scripture are not alike plain in themselves, nor alike clear unto all: yet those things which are necessary to be known, believed, and observed for salvation, are so clearly propounded, and opened in some place of Scripture or other, that not only the learned, but the unlearned, in a due use of the ordinary means, may attain unto a sufficient understanding of them" (WCF 1.7).

6. "Because these original tongues are not known to all the people of God, who have right unto, and interest in the Scriptures, and are commanded, in the fear of God, to read and search them, therefore they are to be translated into the vulgar language of every nation unto which they come, that, the Word of God dwelling plentifully in all, they may worship him in an acceptable manner; and, through patience and comfort of the Scriptures, may have hope" (WCF 1.8).

7. "The infallible rule of interpretation of Scripture is the Scripture itself: and therefore, when there is a question about the true and full sense of any Scripture (which is not manifold, but one), it must be searched and known by other places that speak more clearly" (WCF 1.9).

8. "The supreme judge by which all controversies of religion are to be determined . . . can be no other but the Holy Spirit speaking in the Scripture" (WCF 1.10).

9. WCF 1.5.

10. WCF 1.9.

the ordinary means, may attain unto a sufficient understanding of them.[11]

The Reformation's commitment to *sola Scriptura* was a call to biblical authority and to a biblically defined hermeneutic that resulted in a biblically clear message. This message is the saving work of Christ: "those things which are necessary to be known, believed, and observed for salvation."[12] Thus, the infallible Word when interpreted by its own infallible hermeneutic leads to the clear and saving truth captured by another great Reformation motto: *solus Christus*. The incarnate Word is discovered in the inspired and written Word. While not all of Scripture is equally clear ("all things in Scripture are not alike plain in themselves, nor alike clear unto all"),[13] the glorious redemptive grace found in Jesus Christ is clear even to the untrained student of Scripture ("not only the learned, but the unlearned, in a due use of the ordinary means, may attain unto a sufficient understanding of them").[14]

Thus, it is with sincere gratitude that we recommend to you *Did God Really Say?* and its articles written by scholars from each of the seminaries that we lead. For the sake of the church, these studies present the historically Reformed understanding of the objective and inherent clarity and certainty of the Word of God. Yet they do so while being fully aware of the contemporary milieu of the subjective confusion surrounding so much of recent biblical hermeneutics. The authors are accomplished scholars, and their common concerns reflect the foundational unity of a Christ-centered biblical hermeneutic. This unity stands in spite of their distinctive disciplines and their respective seminary traditions (Westminster, Covenant, Reformed).

11. WCF 1.7.
12. Ibid.
13. Ibid.
14. Ibid.

May Christ's church and Christ's people be strengthened and sharpened in their theology and practice by these contributions. Finally, let us never lose hold of Christ's own claims about Scripture, Scripture's great claims about itself, and Scripture's powerful claims on our lives: "Sanctify them in the truth; your word is truth" (John 17:17); "Let God be true though every one were a liar, as it is written, 'That you may be justified in your words, and prevail when you are judged'" (Rom. 3:4, quoting Ps. 51:4).

Robert C. (Ric) Cannada Jr., Chancellor and CEO, Reformed Theological Seminary

Bryan Chapell, President, Covenant Seminary

Peter A. Lillback, President, Westminster Theological Seminary

January 2012

# Acknowledgments

THE ESSAYS IN *Did God Really Say?* are the fruit of a joint initiative by Covenant Seminary, Reformed Theological Seminary, and Westminster Theological Seminary in Philadelphia, for the Presbyterian Church in America's thirty-ninth General Assembly. Six of these seven essays are written versions of seminar lectures delivered at this General Assembly in Virginia Beach, Virginia, in June 2011. Sincere appreciation goes to Dr. Bryan Chapell, Dr. Ric Cannada, and Dr. Peter Lillback, along with participating faculty from these three seminaries, for their collaboration in this project.

Let me express my appreciation to Michele Saville, Frank Barker III, and the entire Administrative Committee of the Presbyterian Church in America for coordinating, facilitating, and hosting the lectures given at the General Assembly.

Heartfelt thanks go to Steve Bohannon for providing meticulous editorial work, and for giving this consortium volume its useful index and bibliography.

I would also like to thank John Hughes, of P&R Publishing, and Rick Matt for their competency and conscientiousness in bringing this book to its final form.

Finally, thank you to the faithful voices in my ears, encouraging bold engagement with the mounting scholarly and cultural challenges levied against the Word of God. In this regard, special thanks go to my wife, Minda, and to Dr. Richard Gaffin, Dr. Charles

Dunahoo, Dr. Michael Rogers, the Rev. John Currie, the Rev. Dustyn Eudaly, the Rev. Mark Johnston, and again Dr. Peter Lillback, each of whom has, in varying ways, put wind in the sails of this work's fresh articulation of the vital truthfulness and reliability of Scripture. Thank you all for your richly redundant reminders of Paul's recalibrating encouragement to Timothy: "Remember Jesus Christ, risen from the dead, the offspring of David, as preached in my gospel, for which I am suffering, bound with chains as a criminal. But the word of God is not bound!" (2 Tim. 2:8–9).

David B. Garner
January 2012

# Introduction

HISTORY ATTESTS THAT the health of each generation of the church corresponds to its reverence for God's Word. As the view of Scripture goes, so goes the church; as a commitment to God's living Word thrives, God's people thrive. An unswerving reliance upon Scripture produces an active, faithful, vital, and expanding church. When the functional authority of Scripture becomes irrelevant to God's people, the church inescapably abandons its vital mission and becomes an extraneous, spiritually anemic force. The trail to such scriptural neglect exposes various pitfalls into spiritual lethargy.

Passivity, undergirded by an overly optimistic sense of theological stability, has always been among the greatest dangers to the church. Someone once noted, "All that is necessary for the triumph of evil is that good men do nothing."[1] As cursorily compelling as is this sentiment, upholding theological orthodoxy is usually not quite as simple as the courageous actions of "good men" combating conspicuous monstrosities. The triumph of evil more often emerges not because overtly evil men with explicitly evil motives seek subversively evil ends, but because decent men with professedly constructive motives and commendable ends do not perceive the dangers of their views.

1. This quote or some version of it is often attributed to historian Edmund Burke, but it most likely did not come from him. Though the source of the quote is uncertain, its meaning represents a commonly held assumption.

Complicating matters, the contemporary scholar who presents an alternative position often perceives the defense of historic orthodoxy as blindness, stubbornness, ineptitude, naïveté, or even intellectual dishonesty. In fact, many scholars are well convinced that their own views represent theological and orthodox advance, and that their resistant brethren are steeped in an unthinking traditionalism, fearfully ignoring fresh discoveries about Scripture out of complacency or for the sake of blind loyalty to a creed.

In certain cases, they have been right. Traditionalism has hamstrung biblical truth more than once in history. The Reformation rediscovery of the pure gospel of grace and its wise mantra of *semper reformanda* underscore the need for discerning openness. Thus new approaches must neither be welcomed nor rejected in the church simply because they appear new. Fresh ideas, however, must come under the scope of the driving hermeneutical principle well expressed in WCF 1.9, which properly places Scripture itself as the final arbiter and interpreter of truth. Applying this authoritative voice of Scripture remains both vital and vexing.

As centuries of church history bear out, the theological orthodoxy assumed by one generation is the orthodoxy eclipsed by the next. Undiscerning charity fertilizes the seeds of heresy, and the tyranny of all-consuming unbelief is never more than one generation away. Perhaps the greatest threat to theological orthodoxy comes not from those who actively purvey error, but those who seek—for the sake of peace and commendable pastoral graces—a middle road. Puritan Robert Traill brilliantly puts his finger on the psychology of those who seek a compromising synthesis: "such men as are for 'middle ways' in point of doctrine, have usually a greater kindness for that extreme they go half-way *to*, than for that which they go half-way *from*."[2]

Today, so-called evangelical theology seems resolute in showing kindness for what once was called liberalism. To put it frankly, there

2. Recorded in James Buchanan, *The Doctrine of Justification: An Outline of Its History in the Church and Its Exposition from Scripture* (Edinburgh: T&T Clark, 1867), 173.

is an unnerving sympathy within evangelical scholarship for seeking light in darkness, for synthesizing antithesis, and even for wedding belief and unbelief. It has become all too acceptable to appropriate the methods of unbelieving scholarship, to assert common ground with its unbelieving assumptions, and to give such syncretism some credible-sounding, winsome label like "believing criticism."[3] Yet an epistemological, theological, interpretive, or methodological yoke to unbelieving scholarly commitment finds no home in Scripture. "For what partnership has righteousness with lawlessness? Or what fellowship has light with darkness? What accord has Christ with Belial? Or what portion does a believer share with an unbeliever? What agreement has the temple of God with idols?" (2 Cor. 6:14b–16a).

To be sure, preserving theological orthodoxy requires gospel discernment, gospel courage, and gospel grace. It can also be quite lonely. Christian leaders who assess certain controversial formulations as unfortunate and even counterproductive, and even moderates who, in longing for peace, do not usually concern themselves with dividing nuances that seem galactically distant from their practical ministries, may earnestly yearn to believe that their brethren who espouse those controversial formulations would not abandon their theological moorings. Yet the purveyors of new theological perspectives often argue their cases winsomely and can be very persuasive in presenting their resistant rivals as uncharitable. This is nothing new; just remember the case of Athanasius *contra mundum*. Just as she has always done, the church surely must speak to spiritual error courageously and clearly. Yet even the serious stakes do not justify theological rancor; malice and nastiness never represent Christ faithfully. But neither do these stakes warrant a "theology of nice" in the way that political correctness would demand. Our age erroneously caricatures the exposure of errant theology as intrinsically unkind and even un-Christian. The act of simply calling to task gospel error leaves the critic exposed to accusations by many who, while claiming a love for the gospel, betray genuine sympathy only for

3. Kenton L. Sparks, *God's Word in Human Words: An Evangelical Appropriation of Critical Biblical Scholarship* (Grand Rapids: Baker, 2008).

"generous orthodoxy"[4] or some other strained concatenation of biblical terminology and epistemic relativism. To the theological latitudinarians, the only reprehensible position is that of those who call to task their "bad latitude." Despite the protests, overlooking theological error for the sake of superficial peace is both myopic and disobedient. For that matter, neglect of theological error is hardly charitable.

Thus, rigorous and relentless action combined with astutely applied pastoral wisdom is required for every generation of the church. Error arrives surreptitiously and its embryonic forms appear evocatively progressive to some and harmless to most. And by the time theological moderates and peace seekers discern the seriousness of a particular theological error, the battle has usually already been lost. Mainline denominations in the United States of America give ready examples; such history warns us with symphonic eloquence to address with tireless meticulousness even ostensibly minor theological compromises. Passivity ignites error into blazing evil; rest reaps rot, and the consequences of turning our heads in disregard are disastrous.

But reaction *alone* is neither sufficient nor useful. Upholding the truth of the gospel always involves polemics, but never rightly wages war with unbelief without positively proclaiming the glorious and true hope of the gospel. Blazing the pathway for his disciples, Jesus Christ defied the gates of hell to resist his church (Matt. 16:18–20). He made clear that the *way forward* in seasons of theological compromise or spiritual blindness is the *forward way*. That is, while the temptation surges to draw lines in the sand and only to play theological defense, preoccupation with protection alone fosters spiritual atrophy, and all the while fortifies the frequently accurate though painful stereotypes of stodginess and irrelevance, infighting and naval gazing. Defense alone never builds Christ's church. We do the church no service by only fencing ourselves in with theological barricades, acting as sentries at dogmatic gatehouses.

4. See Brian D. McLaren, *Generous Orthodoxy* (El Cajon, CA: Youth Specialties, 2004).

Each generation, building on its forefathers, must seek to restate the truth of Scripture constructively, usefully, and persuasively. We need to rearticulate and celebrate constructive reflections on Scripture. We must preserve and we must promote; we must expose unbelief, and we must express belief. At times rearticulation of theology takes on a polemical face; at other times it takes on a constructive face. But at all times it ought to turn its readers to the face of God in Christ. At all times, the advance of theological truth must undertake just that: gospel advance.

In view of this Christ-centered advancing goal, it might seem odd to title a book on Scripture with words from the archenemy of God himself, the very one who distorts and corrupts God's Word, authors confusion, and leads the masses into damnable darkness. Yet doing so acknowledges the fact that today's *misuse* of God's Word as a method of *undermining* God's Word is neither new nor merely a human endeavor. Though the postmodern age dresses the threats to Scripture somewhat differently, its garments adorn the age-old ploys of the spiritual forces of darkness, whereby the evil one valiantly attempts to lead astray even the elect (Mark 13:22).

When the serpent asks, "Did God actually say?" (Gen. 3:1b), the manner in which he tempts our first parents exposes his consistent *modus operandi*. God's *Word* serves as Satan's point of attack, and twisting and distorting that Word in a way that makes it both familiar and false, he succeeds in deceiving Adam and Eve and their progeny. It is with the Son of God alone that we witness Satan's decisive failure to distort God's Word persuasively, and it is this Son of God who combats the enemy effectively *with the Word of God* (see, e.g., Luke 4:1–11). God's Word purely entreated and directly employed frustrated, disarmed, and ultimately destroyed the tempter.

As Christ relied upon the sufficient, clear, and powerful Word of God, so too must his church, and only in such dependence upon his mighty Word will the church effectively combat the wiles of the enemy. With the force of scriptural authority itself, we turn the question, *Did God Really Say?*, right back on those who continue to misrepresent the gospel with their serpentine-compatible methods. Skepticism about what God really said must be met with fresh enunciation of what *God did really say*.

Committed to Scripture's inherent authority, the authors of this volume have sought to be faithful to the Word of God and thereby faithful to the God of the Word. At places polemical and at places constructive, for the building up of Christ's church, the essays in this volume seek to uphold Scripture faithfully by advancing its authoritative truth.

- In chapter 1, Scott Oliphint addresses our confessional heritage, and builds a strong case for the relevance of the opening chapter of the WCF. Carefully examining the theology of the historic statement itself, Oliphint exposes the two interwoven foundational principles of the Christian faith—the doctrine of God and the doctrine of Scripture, and demonstrates that we must trust Scripture because God is truth itself and Scripture is *his* Word.
- In chapter 2, Michael Williams returns us to a central figure in the development of inerrancy as a doctrine, B. B. Warfield. Soundly rejecting the false caricatures of Warfield and inerrancy, Williams exposes the covenantal contours of biblical inerrancy, noting not only the objective truthfulness of the Word, but also its necessary concomitant, the living faith of God's people.
- In chapter 3, Michael Kruger addresses the popular critiques about the canon of the New Testament, and provides an insightful, accessible, and constructive response to five points of criticism frequently raised. Exposing the assumptions and methods of those critiquing the New Testament canon, he delivers a compelling case for the propriety of the twenty-seven books of the New Testament.
- In chapter 4, Robert Yarbrough puts the language of the 1978 Chicago Statement of Inerrancy into its proper historical and theological framework. He then moves us toward continued positive presentation of the doctrine of Scripture

in this age of unprecedented growth and persecution in the church worldwide, and shows how a proper commitment to a high view of Scripture both characterizes and facilitates the advance of the gospel.

- In chapter 5, Vern Poythress addresses various skeptical theories of language and delivers a strong apologetic for the divine gift of language and the clear voice of God in Scripture. Not only does language have its roots in the Trinity, but God also created this world by speaking. With appreciation for the biblically informed depth of language, Poythress provides responses to current suspicions about metaphor, historical description, stability of meaning, and the philosophical problem of the one and the many.

- In chapter 6, John Frame discusses the contours of N. T. Wright's view of Scripture, highlights points of identification, and underscores some of its doctrinal, epistemological, and functional weaknesses. In the end, Frame calls us to trust in Scripture as the final criterion of truth.

- In chapter 7, I introduce the scope and influence of some contemporary methods of interpretation, and note that, contrary to common contention, biblical clarity is not a product of interpretation but the basis for it. Making a fresh case for an historic doctrine of biblical perspicuity grounded in God's intention to speak to his people, I consider the nature of biblical clarity in view of the unfolding of biblical revelation and how the Holy Spirit's work of illumination coordinates with the clear words of Scripture.

With gratefulness to each contributor, I believe these chapters will draw you to a fresh, informed, and doxological delight in what *God really has said.*

David B. Garner
Westminster Theological Seminary

# Abbreviations

| | |
|---|---|
| *BA* | *Biblical Archaeologist* |
| *BAR* | *Biblical Archaeology Review* |
| *HTR* | *Harvard Theological Review* |
| *I&A* | B. B. Warfield, *The Inspiration and Authority of the Bible*, ed. Samuel G. Craig (Philadelphia: Presbyterian and Reformed, 1948) |
| *Inspiration* | Archibald Hodge and Benjamin B. Warfield, *Inspiration* (Eugene, OR: Wipf and Stock, 2007) |
| *JBL* | *Journal of Biblical Literature* |
| *JBMW* | *Journal for Biblical Manhood and Womanhood* |
| *JETS* | *Journal of the Evangelical Theological Society* |
| *JTS* | *Journal of Theological Studies* |
| *LW* | N. T. Wright, *The Last Word: Scripture and the Authority of God* (San Francisco: HarperSanFrancisco, 2005) |
| PCA | Presbyterian Church in America |
| *PRRD* | Richard A. Muller, *Post-Reformation Reformed Dogmatics: The Rise and Development of Reformed Orthodoxy, ca. 1520 to ca. 1725*, 4 vols. (Grand Rapids: Baker Academic, 1987, 2003) |
| *RB* | *Revue Biblique* |

| | |
|---|---|
| *SC* | N. T. Wright, *Simply Christian: Why Christianity Makes Sense* (San Francisco: HarperSanFrancisco, 2006) |
| *SE* | *Studia Evangelica* |
| *SJT* | *Scottish Journal of Theology* |
| *SSW* | Benjamin B. Warfield, *Benjamin B. Warfield: Selected Shorter Writings*, ed. John E. Meeter, 4th ed., 2 vols. (Phillipsburg, NJ: P&R Publishing, 2001) |
| *StP* | *Studia Patristica* |
| *VC* | *Vigiliae Christianae* |
| *VE* | *Vox Evangelica* |
| WCF | Westminster Confession of Faith |
| *WTJ* | *Westminster Theological Journal* |

# I

# Because It Is the Word of God

K. SCOTT OLIPHINT

MY TASK HERE is to attempt to offer some helpful points with respect to the relationship between our doctrine of Scripture and the first chapter of the WCF. It would be difficult to overestimate the importance of that first chapter. A quick survey of history would show that the church errs and leaves its central task of proclaiming the gospel at precisely the point where it begins to lose its grip on the position articulated in WCF chapter 1, that is, on a *biblical* doctrine of Scripture.

Before looking more specifically at chapter 1, it seems important for the matter at hand to first make clear the *theological* rationale behind the chapter. The question has been asked as to why the confession did not begin with justification, given the central significance of this doctrine during the time of the Reformation, or why it did not begin with Christ, given the centrality of Christology for the Christian faith. We should note here that there was a definite and resolute rationale for beginning this confession with a biblical doctrine of Scripture. In order to understand that rationale, it will help us to remember the deep-seated roots of the theological (and philosophical) notion of *principia*.[1]

## The Principles (*Principia*) of Theology

The term *principia* has its roots in the Greek word *archē* / ἀρχή, which means a beginning point, a source, or a first principle. Its theoretical roots go back at least as far as Aristotle. Aristotle argued that *archai* / ἄρχαι—or first principles, or beginning points—are the "first point from which a thing either is or comes to be or is known."[2] In other words, *archai* / ἄρχαι, according to Aristotle, provide the bedrock foundation for everything that is or is known. This concept of a beginning point, what some have called an Archimedean point, is a necessary and crucial aspect of *all* thinking and being. Aristotle understood this, philosophy has continued to articulate this idea, and Christian theology has seen it as basic to its own discipline.

To use just one example in theology, the Dutch Reformed theologian Sibrandus Lubbertus argued in the late sixteenth century that all disciplines, and especially theology, require *principia*, and that such *principia* partake of at least the following properties: (1) they are necessarily and immutably true, and (2) they must be known *per se*, that is, in themselves, as both immediate and indemonstrable.[3] By "immediate" here is meant that the status of a *principium* is not taken from something external to it, but is inherent in the thing itself. It does not mean, strictly speaking, that nothing *mediated* the truth therein, but rather that nothing *external* mediated that truth. By "indemonstrable" here is meant that the *fact* of a *principium*

1. Here I will depend heavily on the historical spade-work of Richard Muller, but see also Herman Bavinck, *Reformed Dogmatics*, ed. John Bolt, trans. John Vriend, 4 vols. (Grand Rapids: Baker, 1992–2008), 1:205ff.
2. Quoted in Richard A. Muller, *Prolegomena to Theology*, vol. 1 of *PRRD*, 431.
3. Muller, *PRRD*, 1:431.

is not proved by way of syllogism or by external means, but is such that it provides the ground upon which any other fact or demonstration depends. It is, in that sense, as we will see in a minute, a transcendental notion.

For example, speaking of the discipline of theology, Philippe du Plessis-Mornay, the so-called "Huguenot Pope," states:

> For if every science has its *principles*, which it is not lawful to remove, be it ever so little: much more reason is it that it should be so with that thing which hath the ground of all *principles* as its *principle*.[4]

What Mornay says here is not unique among the orthodox Reformed. He is saying much more than that theology has its own *principia*; he was also affirming that, whereas all sciences have their own *principia*, theology's *principia* undergird and underlie any and every other *principia*. The *principia* of other sciences are relative to those sciences; the *principia* of theology are prior to any other *principia* of any and all other disciplines.[5]

For the Reformed, *principia* could never be located, even if tangentially, in the human self. To do so would lead to the kind of skepticism that followed in the wake of Cartesian philosophy. Instead, as Richard Muller notes,

---

4. Philippe du Plessis-Mornay, *A Worke Concerning the Trunesse of Christian Religion, Written in French: Against Atheists, Epicures, Paynims, Iewes, Mahumetists, and Other Infidels. By Philip of Mornay Lord of Plessie Marlie. Begunne to Be Translated into English by That Honourable and Worthy Gentleman, Syr Philip Sidney Knight, and at His Request Finished by Arthur Golding. Since Which Time, It Hath Bene Reviewed, and Is Now the Third Time Published, and Purged from Sundrie Faultes Escaped Heretofore, Thorow Ignorance, Carelesnes, or Other Corruption*, trans. Sir Philip Sidney Knight and Arthur Golding (London: George Eld, 1604), 2, electronic edition accessed through Early English Books Online, http://eebo.chadwyck.com/home.

5. According to Muller, "Divinity alone begins with the absolute first principles of things which depend on no other matters; whereas the basic principles of the other sciences are only first relative to the science for which they provide the foundation, the basic principles of theology are prior to any other 'principle of Being' or 'principle of knowing,'" Muller, *PRRD*, 1:436.

3

The classical philosophical language of *principia* was appropriated by the Reformed orthodox at a time and in a context where . . . [it] served the needs both of the Reformation sense of the priority of Scripture and the Reformation assumptions concerning the ancillary status of philosophy and the weakness of human reason. By defining both Scripture and God as principial in the strictest sense—namely as true, immediate, necessary, and knowable—the early orthodox asserted the priority of Scripture over tradition and reason and gave conceptual status to the notion of its self-authenticating character in response to both Roman polemicists and philosophical skeptics of the era.[6]

We should make clear here that in Reformed thinking there were two *principia*, and this follows again from philosophical discussions dating at least as far back as Aristotle. In *Metaphysics* 4.3, Aristotle notes that first principles, in order to be *first* principles, must themselves be most certain, indemonstrable, immediately evident, and *never* a postulate or hypothesis. According to Aristotle, first principles are that which anyone must have when he comes to study anything at all. First principles, therefore, cannot be something that someone acquires as a result of one's reasoning or argument.

In this sense, as we just mentioned, the *principia* that form the foundation for everything else are themselves transcendental in nature. They provide for the possibility of anything else; if in a particular science, then they provide for the possibility of that science. But if in an ultimate sense, as is the case with theological *principia*, then they provide for the possibility of anything else whatsoever. They provide for the possibility of *being* and for the possibility of *knowing*.

## GOD AND HIS WORD

This brings us to a further general point concerning *principia* that relates directly to our confessional study. In the discussions of

6. Ibid., 432.

*principia*, two categories were central. Again, following on philo-sophical concerns, *principia* were referenced to two central contexts. There was necessarily a *principium* with respect to Being and, just as necessarily, a *principium* with respect to knowing. *Principia*, therefore, refer primarily to the *principium essendi*, which is the principle, source, or foundation of Being, and the *principium cogno-scendi*, which is the principle, source, or foundation of knowing.

Given these two concerns, the two primary doctrines that serve as *principia* for theology are the doctrine of God and the doctrine of Scripture. And while we do not have the space here to work out the relationship between these two *principia*, we should note at least the following.

First, the juxtaposition, so familiar in the Reformed confessions, between the doctrine of Scripture and the doctrine of God relates specifically to a particular Reformed understanding of who God is and of how he may be known. One of Calvin's brightest students, Franciscus Junius, developed a categorization of the knowledge of God that relates directly to the Reformed scholastic understanding of *principia*.

In attempting to articulate the relationship of God's own knowledge to our knowledge of God, Junius made a distinction between archetypal knowledge and ectypal knowledge. Archetypal knowledge is that knowledge that God alone has. It is knowledge of God that partakes of all the essential divine attributes. Hence, it is knowledge that just *is* God himself, given the simplicity of God.

Ectypal knowledge is true knowledge that has its foundation in archetypal knowledge. Notice that this knowledge is not identical with God's archetypal knowledge. It could not be since archetypal knowledge is infinite, eternal, immutable, etc. But it is nevertheless *true* knowledge, even though finite and limited, because it has its roots in God's own essential knowledge. God himself has ectypal knowledge, based on his archetypal knowledge, and God's ectypal knowledge is given to his creatures by way of revelation; we then also have ectypal knowledge.

This is all just another way of saying that the only way in which we can know God, or anything else, is if God graciously chooses to reveal himself to us. As creatures, therefore—and this is the salient point to make with respect to the Reformed confessions, and the WCF particularly—there is an inextricable *principial* link between God and revelation. From the perspective of the creature, we cannot have one without the other.

It was this concern, the concern for *principia*, as those relate specifically to God and our knowledge of him, that brought about a specifically Reformed doctrine of Scripture. Prior to the Reformation, there is no well-articulated doctrine of Scripture, especially a doctrine of Scripture that fills the place of a *principium cognoscendi*. While Aquinas and Duns Scotus note the necessity of revelation, neither of them develops a doctrine of Scripture as a *principium* of theology.[7]

What we have, therefore, in this most excellent beginning chapter from the WCF is something solidly Reformed, magnificently creative (in the best sense), and theologically (as well as philosophically) charged. What we have is an articulation and a true "confession" of what are for Reformed folk our bedrock foundations, Scripture and God, apart from which we cannot know anything, without which we cannot have any certainty, and behind which we cannot go.

## Because It Is the Word of God

I would like now to set out just a highlight or two from chapter 1 of the WCF. We can begin by remembering the historical moment of its composition. According to B. B. Warfield, who quotes noted church historian and WCF scholar Alex F. Mitchell:

> "If any chapter of the Westminster Confession of Faith," says Prof. Mitchell, "was framed with more elaborate care than another, it was that which treats 'Of the Holy Scripture.' It was considered paragraph by paragraph—almost clause by clause—by the House

7. This point is taken from Richard A. Muller, *Holy Scripture: The Cognitive Foundation of Theology*, vol. 2 of *PRRD*, 152.

of Commons, as well as by the Assembly of Divines, before it was finally passed."[8]

Warfield goes on to note that, in spite of the care given to this chapter, there was very little debate about its content; the divines were, as he says, "very much at one concerning its propositions." The reason for this is fairly clear. By the time the Assembly met to put together the confession, the nature of Scripture, particularly with respect to a *doctrine* of Scripture, was not a controversial issue among Protestants.

Sadly, such is not the case in our own day. Especially with the rise of new forms of theology set forth today, subtle attacks on the doctrine of Scripture as presented in chapter 1 of the confession are proliferating. In order to understand these attacks, we should be clear about the relationship between Scripture itself and our confession.

## Scripture as Norming Norm

One way (maybe not the best way) to think of this relationship is by way of a classical, categorical distinction between the *norma normans* and the *norma normata*. In this distinction, Scripture is the *norma normans*, or the norming norm, whereas the WCF is the *norma normata*, or the normed norm. The confession takes its cue from Scripture; embedded in the confession is the theology of Scripture itself. Since, therefore, Scripture is the original authority and is the Word of God, it alone should be seen to be infallible and inspired. The norm that is normed *by Scripture*, that is, the confession, has its authority derivatively; it is not authoritative because of what it is in itself, as is Scripture, but because of its origin. That is, its authority obtains only when and where it is in conformity to Scripture. Unlike Scripture, therefore, the confession is a derivative and fallible document.

8. B. B. Warfield, "The Westminster Doctrine of Holy Scripture," in *SSW*, 2:560.

## The Short Step

It is a short step, however, from this truth to its perversion. It is a short step, though we must admit a short *distorted* step, from the affirmation of the confession's fallibility to an affirmation of its functional uselessness. One example will have to suffice here, an example that is given on a more "popular" level and therefore has the double implication of being both superficial and, perhaps for that reason, more influential. In one recent criticism of a confessional approach to theology, the author notes the following:

> Such an approach [that is, a traditional confessional approach to theology] is characteristic among those who hold confessional statements in an absolutist fashion and claim such statements teach the "system" of doctrine contained in Scripture. [It should not escape us here that the author, in this statement, has just indicted the entirety of Reformed and Presbyterian churches.] The danger here is that such a procedure can hinder the ability to read the text and to listen to the Spirit in new ways.[9]

This criticism, we should note is couched in terminology that would be appealing to some, especially to some who look askance at Reformed theology. It is couched in terms that require *either* that one is confessional, or that one is spiritual, i.e., "listening to the Spirit in new ways." This "necessarily provisional dimension" of theology accrues, we are told, to any and every doctrine that is gleaned from Scripture.[10]

It should be noted, however, that this way of construing the relationship of doctrine, and particularly of confessional doctrine, to Scripture gets things backwards. In our affirmation of the full, unique, divine authority of Scripture, and of the consequent possible

---

9. John Franke, *The Character of Theology: An Introduction to Its Nature, Task, and Purpose* (Grand Rapids: Baker Academic, 2005), 135.

10. See as well John R. Franke, "Reforming Theology: Toward a Postmodern Reformed Dogmatics," *WTJ* 65, 1 (Spring 2003): 1–26.

fallibility of every human construction of doctrine, we are *not* at the same time affirming that everything to which we confessional folk subscribe is *only* and always provisional; fallibility and provisionality are *not* two sides of the same coin. I am a fallible human being, prone to sin and limited in everything that I think and do. But that fact does not in any way cause me to lack certainty in the fact that I am now typing these words in my study. Neither should it cause you to lack certainty that you are where you are and are reading these very words. Neither does it cause me to lose certainty about that fact that Christ is the Son of God, the second person of the Trinity, who took on a human nature, or that the triune God exists, or that Jesus Christ is the only way to the Father. These are theological construals, but I am nevertheless certain of their truth. I do not hold such truths provisionally. Fallibility does not *entail* provisionality.

By the same token, the relationship of Scripture to the truth set forth in the confession is not such that we affirm that the Holy Spirit has completed his work of illumination in the church (as if nothing new could be gleaned from Holy Scripture). It goes without saying that an affirmation of truth, even of *much* truth, is not, thereby, an affirmation of *all* truth. Thus these kinds of approaches have yet to work through the most basic issues of what it means to be confessional.

**Confessing Biblical Truth**

What we confess in our Confession is that a particular confession contains nothing less than biblical truth. What we are confessing, in other words (in words taken from chapter 1 of this very confession), is that, in our subscribing to this confession, we are agreeing that what it articulates, is, *by good and necessary consequence*, the very truth of God himself, revealed in Scripture, and systematically articulated in the confession.

A brief word about the phrase *good and necessary consequence*. Suppose I am your pastor, and I say to you that a consequence of the biblical command to love your neighbor is that you should be involved, at least voluntarily, in some kind of social mission work each week. You ask me why I would assert such a thing and I say that it follows from the command to love your neighbor. Am I right? Does it follow? It certainly does. But just because it follows from that command does not mean that it is entailed by that command. That is, social work is a *good* consequence of the command to love your neighbor, but it is not a necessary one. To make it a necessary consequence would have the effect of adding a specific command to Scripture.

On the other hand, what if you and I are involved in a Bible study together, and we begin our study with the doctrine of God. We look through Scripture and, after much searching and exegetical work, conclude that when Scripture speaks of the Father it is speaking of God, when it speaks of the Son it is speaking of God, and when it speaks of the Holy Spirit it is speaking of God. The Father has distinct properties, so does the Son, so does the Spirit. What, then, is the necessary consequence of such a study? It is that these three distinct individuals are all three God. Does that mean that there are three Gods? That may be a *necessary* consequence of our study, but it cannot be a *good* consequence, because Scripture will not allow such a conclusion. So, though the fact that the three Persons are distinct, with properties unique to each, and are also all three fully and completely God might *entail* the fact that there are three Gods, Scripture will not allow for such a conclusion. It is not a *good* consequence in that it does not conform to what Scripture requires us to affirm. We affirm, therefore, that God is one in essence and three in Persons; he is both One and Three.

But here is the point with regard to confessions. Is it the case that your affirmation of the Trinity, or mine, is simply a fallible, provisional, "restricting-of-the-Spirit" kind of affirmation? This has not been the church's practice with regard to such a confession. You cannot be a member of a Reformed or Presbyterian church (that is, a *biblical* Reformed or Presbyterian church) unless you confess in some credible way the triune God, and unless that confession carries with it the content and authority of Scripture itself. That is, your confession is a confession of *your faith*, of the faith as it is set down for us in Scripture, which you have embraced. Or, to put it in more practical terms, once you begin to question the doctrine of the Trinity, any church worth its biblical salt will need to address those questions with you, especially in terms of your membership in that church.

To put it in the context of our discussion of *principia*, if current trends that seek to deny confessional commitment are correct, and if everything is necessarily provisional, then there really are no *principia*, no true, certain, immediate, and indemonstrable principles on which we all must stand. But of course, if that is true, then either Scripture is not infallible, or, if infallible, there is no way for us to access it, since we are all confined within our own contextual or linguistic cocoons. But then, if that is true, not only is everything that we say floating in the air, without grounding or foundation, but there simply is no truth to be had at all. No *principia* means no truth, or at least no knowledge of the truth. The only upside to this is that the notion that everything is contextual and provisional is itself floating in the air, and should be taken no more seriously than anything else.

The first chapter of the WCF is designed to negate such approaches, and to provide parameters within which we can operate. WCF chapter 1 lays out for us the reality of our *principium cognoscendi*; it gives us, in a way that is without equal in the history of the church, a robust and lively doctrine of Scripture. It articulates where it is that Christians stand with respect to that which they claim to know and believe.

## THE AUTHORITY OF SCRIPTURE

With that in mind, we can focus the discussion on the notion of the authority of Scripture as the confession lays it out for us.

First, a minor point or two with respect to the authority of Scripture. While this is a minor *point*, we should not think that what the Westminster divines did here was a minor *matter*.

After laying out the *necessity* of Scripture—a necessity, we should note, that has its foundation in, as the confession says, the good pleasure of God—the divines provide an itemization of the books of Scripture in section 2. That is, after affirming that it pleased the Lord to have written down what he, at other times and places, chose to reveal in various ways, the confession lays out for us the parts of the whole and affirms those parts to be "given by inspiration of God to be the rule of faith and life." Then section 3, in case there be any misunderstanding, goes on to affirm that the apocryphal books, "not being of divine inspiration, are no part of the canon of the Scripture."

The reason for sections 2 and 3 is important for our discussion of authority. The so-called "formal principle" of debate during the time of the Reformation was the issue of Scripture, more generally the issue of authority itself. So why spell out each and every book of the Bible? One reason would be that the Council of Trent had done just that, with different results. As a matter of fact, according to Richard Muller, "Beginning with the fourth session of the Council of Trent in 1546 . . . *for the first time in the history of the church* . . . the canon of Scripture received not only clear identification and enumeration but also confessional and dogmatic definition."[11]

Because the issue at the time of the Reformation, including the issue debated during the Counter-Reformation, was the issue of authority, the Council of Trent thought it necessary to enumerate both the books of Scripture and the "official" version of Scripture in the Latin Vulgate. But the books enumerated by Trent are different from the ones enumerated in the WCF.

What should be underscored here is that it is not the case simply that Protestants have a different canon of Scripture than Romanists. That is true enough. But what should be seen, and what is

---

11. Muller, *PRRD*, 2:372 (emphasis added).

more fundamental, is that the Council of Trent determined not that the books of Scripture would be different *simpliciter* (simply), but that the Roman church would itself *be canon*, the normative rule of faith and practice, for the Roman church. So the issue is not simply which books are included; the issue is *why* the books that are included are included. For the Romanists, the books included are included because the church says so.[12]

It is not the case, therefore, that Scripture is the *principium* for the Roman church. Rather, with regard to the formal principle of the Reformation, two vastly different notions of *principium cognoscendi* emerged. The Roman view is that holy mother church, and it alone, is the true, immediate, and indemonstrable *principium*. This is why a *fides implicita* (implicit faith) is the proper response of those within that church. For the Reformed, however, because Scripture is inspired, it provides its own criteria for canon, and thus is its own self-referential authority.

And this leads us to the major point articulated in section 4 of the WCF. After establishing the *necessity* of Scripture in section 1, and the content of Scripture in sections 2 and 3, section 4 declares the self-referential authority, what we might call the *principial* authority, of Holy Scripture:

> The authority of the Holy Scripture, for which it ought to be believed, and obeyed, dependeth not upon the testimony of any man, or Church; but wholly upon God (who is truth itself) the author thereof: and therefore it is to be received, because it is the Word of God.

One of the first things that must be firmly embedded in our minds in this regard is the absolute self-attesting authority of Scripture. You can, no doubt, understand some of the reasons

---

12. It is worth noting here that the Romanist notion is circular; it declares itself to be its own final authority. The problem, though, is not circularity *per se*; the problem is which circle is the proper one. Rome thinks its circle is proper, based on itself. Historically, the only options available are either that the church is the final authority (thus, authority depends on man) or that Scripture is.

for that, particularly in the face of opposition from Roman Catholicism.

Notice first of all, that the confession is interested specifically here in *authority*, the authority of Scripture. And the intent of the paragraph is to set out for us the *ground* as to why the Scriptures are *authoritative*, and thus why they ought to be believed and obeyed. The section sets out very clearly that the authority of Scripture in no way rests on the church or its councils, or on any man. Rather, its authority rests on its author, God, and is to be received because it is his Word. This is sometimes called the *autopiston* of Scripture, translated as self-attesting, or self-authenticating. What does that mean?

### The Self-Attestation of Scripture

We should be clear that self-attestation *does not* mean self-evident. Self-authentication, or attestation, is an objective attribute, whereas self-evident refers more specifically to the knowing agent. It therefore does *not* mean that revelation as self-authenticated compels agreement. That which is self-authenticating can be denied. What it means is that it *needs* no other authority as confirmation in order to be justified and absolutely authoritative in what it says. This does *not* mean that nothing else attends that authority; there are other evidences, which we will see in a moment. What it *does* mean is that nothing else whatsoever is needed, nor is there anything else that is able to supersede this ground, in order for Scripture to be deemed authoritative. To put the matter philosophically, Scripture's warrant rests solely and completely in itself, *because of what it is*, the very Word of God.

This is why we must understand the nature of a *principium* in order to see what the Westminster divines were doing in this chapter. Again, according to Muller,

> Since . . . it is of the very nature of a first principle that it is most certain, indemonstrable or immediately evident, and never a

postulate or hypothesis, the Reformed orthodox identification of Scripture as the *principium cognoscendi unicum*[13] of theology involves the assumption that the biblical norm cannot be rationally or empirically verified and, indeed, need not be—and that its authority is known in and through its self-authenticating character.[14]

The confession is quite perspicuous at this point. When the question comes as to the ground or foundation of Scripture's authority, the divines knew that to reference anything other than Scripture would be to deny the Word of God as theological *principium*. They knew this because the only other option available, and the prime example of this—the Roman Catholic church—was right before their eyes. And note the juxtaposition of the two *principia* of theology embedded within this one section. The authority of Scripture depends on God, who is truth itself, and therefore is to be received because it is his Word. Not because we say it is his Word or have shown it to be his Word, but because of what it *is*, the very Word of God. Self-attestation is embedded authority.

We should note here that the point made in section 4 of the confession is not *simply* that Scripture is the Word of God because it says it is. Rather, the point is that Scripture is the Word of God because God, who is truth itself, is its author. This is an important point in the face of other, false, religions that also have books that claim to have come from God or to be his word. Many of those books were around during the writing of this confession; the divines were aware of such things.

The point the confession is making, however, is simply that God has worked in a particular way in history, revealing himself through various means along the way, and that now, since it has pleased him to commit such revelation to writing, he himself has authored Holy Scripture. It is incumbent on those who hear it or read it, therefore, to receive it because it is God himself speaking in and through every word of it.

13. "Only source of knowing."
14. Muller, *PRRD*, 1:436–37.

In his discussion on the authority of Scripture, Calvin says this:

> It is utterly vain then to pretend that the power of judging Scripture so lies with the church that its certainty depends upon churchly assent. Thus, while the church receives and gives its seal of approval to the Scriptures, it does not thereby render authentic what is otherwise doubtful or controversial. But because the church recognizes Scripture to be the truth of its own God, as a pious duty it unhesitatingly venerates Scripture. As to their question [thinking here of the Roman Catholic doctrines]—How can we be assured that this has sprung from God unless we have recourse to the decree of the church?—it is as if someone asked: Whence will we learn to distinguish light from darkness, white from black, sweet from bitter? Indeed, Scripture exhibits fully as clear evidence of its own truth as white and black things do of their color, or sweet and bitter things do of their taste.[15]

Calvin later declares that Scripture is self-authenticated. "Hence," says Calvin, "it is not right to subject it to proof or reasoning."[16] This is, by definition, a *principium*. Calvin affirms that there is no higher authority to which one can appeal for proof, no better or more transcendent reasoning, than looking to Scripture itself, since it carries with it its own infallible authority. Any other reasoning, any other proof, will simply be subject to error and confusion. The basic principle of self-attestation is that we understand what Scripture *is* by subjecting it to itself, and to itself alone. It is *its own* witness, by virtue of what it is.

## The Author of Scripture

We have one further point to make on this section, a point that could easily be overlooked but that is prescient in its affirmation, given current discussions of Scripture. Note that this section, which

15. John Calvin, *Institutes of the Christian Religion*, ed. John T. McNeill, trans. Ford Lewis Battles, 2 vols. (Philadelphia: Westminster, 1975), 1.7.2.
16. Ibid., 1.7.5.

is the only section that references the authorship of Scripture, says that Scripture has *one* author, and that its author is God.

For the Reformed, God, and God alone, is *the* author of Scripture. It is surely not the case that the Westminster divines were unaware of the fact that God used men to write his own Word. But they were jealous to maintain that, even though men were used to write God's Word down, those men were not, in the fullest sense of the word, *authors*. Men used to write God's Word were the *ministers*, used by God. Scripture's author is God, who uses "actuaries" or "tabularies" to write his words. If the notion of authorship can be used with respect to these men they were themselves *instrumental* secondary authors.[17] Or, to use the causal language in use during this time, men were *instrumental* causes while God, and God alone, was the *efficient* cause of Scripture, and therefore could be referenced as *the* author of Scripture.

*God* is the primary author of Scripture, and men are instrumental secondary authors. And, if instruments, then what men write down is as much God's own words as if he had written it down without human mediation. We should not lose sight of the fact that this section notes that Scripture's author is God, not God and man. This notion of divine authorship is in keeping with the Scripture's notion of itself, i.e., that it is *theopneustos* ("God-breathed," 2 Tim. 3:16); it is not *theo-* and *anthropopneustos* ("man-breathed").

In other words, what the confession sets out to affirm here is that Scripture is *foundationally* and *essentially* divine. In this entire chapter on the doctrine of Scripture, there is no mention of the human authors of Scripture. This is no oversight in the confession; it is not that the Reformers and their progeny did not recognize the

17. Muller observes that "the Protestant scholastics looked both to the medieval scholastic tradition and to the works of the Reformers. From the medieval teachers they received the definition of God as the *auctor principalis sive primarius Scripturae* and of human beings, the prophets and apostles, as secondary authors or instruments. From the Reformers they received no new language, but they did find confirmation of the point in the repeated identification of Scripture as God's Word, as given by God." Muller, *PRRD*, 2:226.

human element of Scripture. It is not that they were not privy to extra-biblical sources and other cultural, contextual, and human elements that surround Scripture. Rather, it is in keeping with the testimony of Scripture itself about itself that the WCF affirms that Scripture is foundationally and essentially divine (though contingently, secondarily, and truly human).[18] This means for the WCF (and Reformed theology faithful to it) that the *doctrine* of Scripture is to be formulated and framed *first of all* according to *itself* as God's Word (i.e., its *self*-witness).[19] The confession is setting forth the notion here, radical in its context, that one determines *what* Scripture is not by going somewhere outside of Scripture, but by *Scripture itself*. It carries its authority and its "doctrine" within itself. We come again to the notion of Scripture as the *principium cognoscendi*.

Second, and building on the first point, the divines understood that we cannot allow the so-called "phenomena" of Scripture, as important as those phenomena are, to establish a *doctrine* of Scripture, or to determine just what Scripture *is*. This principle is well articulated by B. B. Warfield. Speaking of the human writers of Holy Scripture, Warfield notes:

> If they are trustworthy teachers of doctrine and if they held and taught this doctrine (i.e., of inspiration), then this doctrine is true, and is to be accepted and acted upon as true by us all. In that case, *any objections brought against the doctrine from other spheres of enquiry are inoperative*; it being a settled logical principle that so long as the proper evidence by which a proposition is established remains unrefuted, all so-called objections [based on the data or "phenomena" of Scripture] brought against it [Scripture's self-

18. "[The] distinction between revelation and inspiration is also demanded by the Reformed assumption that, 'considered essentially,' Scripture proceeds from God, while 'accidentally,' it was written by human beings." Ibid., 242.

19. According to Richard Muller: "The entire discussion [of the causes of Scripture] appears to be an outgrowth of the language of Scripture as the *self-authenticating* and *self-interpreting* ultimate norm for faith and practice—and, therefore, the *sole norm* for the framing of a doctrine of Scripture." Ibid., 230 (emphasis added).

witness] pass out of *the category of objections* to its truth into *the category of difficulties to be adjusted to it. . . .* The really decisive question among Christian scholars (among whom alone, it would seem, could a question of inspiration be profitably discussed), is thus seen to be, "What does an exact and scientific exegesis determine to be the Biblical doctrine of Inspiration?"[20]

This is how we understand Scripture's authority, its inspiration and its self-witness.

In another place, in speaking of the WCF's doctrine of Scripture, Warfield notes the view of John Lightfoot, one of the divines of Westminster. According to Lightfoot, the phenomena of Scripture, which can cause difficulty of understanding, are there, at least in part, for that reason. Commenting on 2 Peter 3:15, John Lightfoot notes Peter's admission that some things in Paul are hard to understand. This, however, does not mean that Scripture's authority is in question, as if our understanding of it were a condition of that authority. Rather, says Lightfoot, Peter

> acknowledges that in some places [the Scriptures] are hard to be understood, and were misconstrued by some unlearned and unstable ones, to their own ruin; yet neither doth he nor Paul, who was yet alive and well knew of this wresting of his Epistles, clear or amend those difficulties, but let them alone as they were: for the Holy Ghost hath so penned Scripture as to set men to study.[21]

This is what it means for Scripture to be its own witness; this is what it means that Scripture is to be believed and obeyed because it is the Word of God. Any other "because" that would be inserted, if thought to be a final court of appeal, would undermine the

20. B. B. Warfield, *The Inspiration and Authority of the Bible* (Philadelphia: Presbyterian and Reformed, 1948), 174–75 (emphasis added).

21. John Lightfoot, *The Harmony, Chronicle, and Order of the New Testament*, vol. 3 of *The Whole Works of the Reverend and Learned John Lightfoot*, ed. John Rogers Pitman (London: J. F. Dove, 1822), 327, quoted in B. B. Warfield, *The Westminster Assembly and Its Work* (New York: Oxford University Press, 1931), 296.

Reformed principle of *sola Scriptura*. It would undermine Scripture's self-attestation. It would undermine the fact of Scripture's essential divinity. This is the note sounded by the apostle in his assessment of his own preaching, an assessment that is directly applicable to Scripture as a whole, that, ultimately considered, it is to be received "not as the word of man, but as what it really [alēthōs / ἀληθῶς] is, the word of God" (1 Thess. 2:13).

One final point before we conclude. Nothing we have said thus far means that Scripture does not carry anything else with it to testify of its own character. Self-authentication, self-attestation, does not simply exist in a vacuum.

In line with this, and clearly with this in mind, chapter 1 of the WCF, after affirming Scripture's self-attestation, continues in this way in section 5:

> We may be moved and induced by the testimony of the Church to an high and reverent esteem of the Holy Scripture. And the heavenliness of the matter, the efficacy of the doctrine, the majesty of the style, the consent of all the parts, the scope of the whole (which is, to give all glory to God), the full discovery it makes of the only way of man's salvation, the many other incomparable excellencies, and the entire perfection thereof, are arguments whereby it does abundantly evidence itself to be the Word of God: yet notwithstanding, our full persuasion and assurance of the infallible truth and divine authority thereof, is from the inward work of the Holy Spirit bearing witness by and with the Word in our hearts.

The point here, perhaps a minor point, though a major truth, is that the arguments and evidence available to show that Scripture is authored by God, that it attests to its own authority, that it is the *principium cognoscendi*, is found, as we should expect by now, in Scripture itself. Scripture's authority, therefore, is not established by man nor given by man, but is intrinsic to its character because of its source. Scripture is essentially authoritative; that is its nature, and there is abundant evidence for that authority.

## CONCLUSION

We may, no doubt, be frustrated that we have not given such a magnificent and majestic chapter its due. We certainly have not. What we have attempted to do, however, is to argue that the structure of this chapter is such that Reformed Christians who subscribe to this confession are thereby bound to affirm the reality and the necessity of theological *principia*. This affirmation will have at least two positive applications for us.

The first is that we will, of necessity, hold the Word of God high as our sole ground for a redemptive knowledge of God (and of everything else). This has the practical effect of helping us to understand just why it is that those outside of Christ must be, as Paul says, "renewed unto knowledge."

One short example of how this might go wrong will help illustrate the point. In a book designed to help readers rethink their doctrine of Scripture, one author contends that due to the humanness of Scripture, any cohesive or coherent understanding of what the Bible says betrays what it, in fact, *is*. So, to attempt to understand how it can be that God is both eternal and that he, for example, interacts with us in time is to do an injustice to what Scripture *is*, it is to deny its humanness, or so we are told. But in arguing against the coherence of Scripture, the author notes that whether or not prayer has "some effect on God" is "for God to know, not us."[22] In this way of thinking, the very reality of prayer has to be reconstrued as an act of agnosticism, because Scripture is so diverse that we could never conjure up a coherent understanding of an eternal and immutable God who actually hears and responds to our prayers. Is there any question, given this example, of just how inextricably linked the *principium cognoscendi* is to the *principium essendi*? The doctrine of Scripture presented here is no abstract doctrine, but is the only way in which we can begin rightly to see who God is and how we might properly worship him.

22. Peter Enns, *Inspiration and Incarnation* (Grand Rapids: Baker Academic, 2005), 107.

The second application of this confessional understanding of what Scripture is will have the effect of solidifying for us the fact that unless Christianity be true, unless, that is, the Reformed doctrine of God and of Scripture as the two inextricably linked *principia* be affirmed, then nothing can either be or be true. This means that revelation must be the ground for everything else that we know, in theology and in any other sphere of life. That, in itself, is fundamental to a Reformed understanding of theology. Without revelation as our *principium*, we have no foundation or ground for any knowledge, including, but not limited to, our knowledge of God in Christ.

# 2

# The Church, a Pillar of Truth: B. B. Warfield's Church Doctrine of Inspiration

MICHAEL D. WILLIAMS

PERHAPS NO CHRISTIAN doctrine is so identified with a single man's name as is that of the inerrancy of Scripture with B. B. Warfield. At a time in which belief in the divine authorship of the Bible was being abandoned as quickly as it was being questioned within critical circles, Warfield's learned and dogged defense of the Bible as the Word of God would set the parameters of the debate for a century of evangelical Christians. In giving us an eloquent and powerful apologetic for the divine inspiration of Scripture, Warfield would do more than any other writer to shape, explain, and defend the evangelical understanding of the Bible as the Word of God.

Quite simply, whether one agrees with him or not, Warfield gets a seat at the table for any discussion of the doctrine of the inspiration of Scripture. Yet while both his friends and critics alike admit that

23

his is an essential voice, many seem not to have read him, or have read only snippets of his work quoted by other authors. Warfield's construction of the doctrine of inerrancy has been particularly ripe for easy characterization, even caricature, especially by those who dislike the doctrine.[1] One does not have to look far to find Warfield's defense of the Bible as the Word of God described as deductivist, scholastic, and rationalistic, the product of Enlightenment objectivism[2] and dogmatic obscurantism.[3] Even among those who affirm the Bible as the divinely authoritative and inspired Word of God, Warfield's construction is sometimes demeaned as dispassionate, spiritless, "cold and clinical."[4]

I believe that these depictions are unfair to both Warfield and his doctrine of Scripture, but I can understand how one can reach

1. Noting George Hunsinger's depiction of Karl Barth as having "achieved the dubious distinction of being habitually honored but not much read," Raymond D. Cannata ironically turns the comment on Warfield, who "has achieved the more dubious distinction of being habitually *dis*honored and not much read." Raymond D. Cannata, "Warfield and the Doctrine of Scripture," in *B. B. Warfield: Essays on His Life and Thought*, ed. Gary L. W. Johnson (Phillipsburg, NJ: P&R Publishing, 2007), 97.

2. G. C. Berkouwer, *Holy Scripture* (Grand Rapids: Eerdmans, 1975), 181–84, introduces his own treatment of inerrancy with a footnote more or less assigning the doctrine to Warfield and then attaching a short list of sound-bite-like Warfield quotations. The doctrine of inerrancy is, in Berkouwer's estimation, an illegitimate search for rational exactness and results in a conception of the Bible that is decidedly "dualistic" (docetist). Warfield, however, explicitly and repeatedly rejected both of these notions, and in my estimation cannot be said to be guilty of either.

3. For example, Ernest R. Sandeen claimed that Warfield set up a formal doctrine of inspiration, and made it dependent upon external evidences in such a manner as to render void the traditional Reformed doctrine of the testimony of the Spirit. See his *The Roots of Fundamentalism: British and American Millenarianism, 1800–1930* (Chicago: University of Chicago Press, 1970), 118–21. In a footnote, Sandeen went so far as to allege that the Princetonian use of the term *inerrancy* as a way of describing biblical truth-telling is inherently rationalistic (125n40). See John D. Woodbridge and Randal H. Balmer, "The Princetonians and Biblical Authority: An Assessment of the Ernest Sandeen Proposal," in *Scripture and Truth*, ed. D. A. Carson and John D. Woodbridge (Grand Rapids: Baker, 1983), 254–69, and John H. Gerstner, "Warfield's Case for Biblical Inerrancy," in *God's Inerrant Word*, ed. John W. Montgomery (Newburgh, IN: Trinity Press, 1974), 116–20, for responses to Sandeen.

4. E.g., A. T. B. McGowan, *The Divine Authenticity of Scripture: Retrieving an Evangelical Heritage* (Downers Grove, IL: InterVarsity Press, 2007), 117.

these sorts of conclusions if one has read only bits and pieces of Warfield or is unaware of Warfield's apologetic and historical moment. I especially think that the caricatures of Warfield are cogent when we understand that they are often not about him at all. Those who have followed in the tradition of Hodge and Warfield have often sought to capture their approach toward the Bible in short, almost creedal statements, which, while true, often give no evidence of Scripture's import to the life of faith.[5] As an example, note the creedal statement of the Evangelical Theological Society: "The Bible alone, and the Bible in its entirety, is the Word of God written and is therefore inerrant in the autographs." True enough, but not *enough*. I agree with the statement as far as it goes, but I want more. Warfield certainly would have agreed with it, but wanted a lot more, and said a lot more.

In a 2007 collection of essays on Warfield's life and thought, Moisés Silva acknowledged the legacy of B. B. Warfield and his doctrine of inerrancy in shaping the history and ethos of Westminster Theological Seminary. "It may be an exaggeration, but only a mild one," writes Dr. Silva, "to say that the infallibility of Scripture, with its implications, has provided Westminster's *raison d'être*. Indeed, as far as the present faculty is concerned, we would sooner pack up our books than abandon our conviction that the

---

5. Timothy Ward notes that the rush to form neat systematic statements sometimes comes at the cost of existential payout. When the hard-won exegetical and theological conclusion of one generation becomes the dogmatic assertion or starting point of the next, the urgency and importance of the issue might very well be lost. "The evangelical doctrine of Scripture seemed to many to have become lifeless, devoid of the explicit deep biblical and theological roots that need to remain in place in order to give it spiritual vitality. In fact it is arguable that many who have come to reject the evangelical doctrine of Scripture have done so not so much because they have just found it to be wrong biblically or intellectually incredible, but because they have found the expositions of it which they know of to be lacking in what we might call dynamic spirituality. In the writing of theology there is indeed a need for careful precision; there should also be times when the doctrine is related directly to Christian life and hope lived out in relationship with God." Timothy Ward, *Words of Life: Scripture as the Living and Active Word of God* (Downers Grove, IL: InterVarsity Press, 2009), 51.

Scriptures are truly God's very breath."[6] That last sentence is *crucial*, and Warfield would have affirmed it wholeheartedly. There is an inescapable subjective aspect to the doctrine of inerrancy. I might even say that it is the heart of the matter, as it touches upon the essential question of how the people of God are to approach, read, and proclaim the Word.

Here then is my thesis: Although it is usually missed, Warfield's understanding of the Bible as God's inerrantly true Word assumes a covenantal understanding of Scripture. That is to say, the doctrine of Scripture includes both a divine speaker or initiator and a community of hearers or respondents. Once we push past the easy slogans relative to the doctrine of inerrancy and factor in the historical-apologetic moment of Warfield's contribution and his own distinctive language and constructs, it becomes clear that his understanding of the inerrancy of Scripture demands a subjective component: the people of God who believe, submit to, and proclaim the Bible as the Word of God. To say it a bit differently, the doctrine of inerrancy is not only about the truthfulness of the Spirit-inspired Word but also about the trust a Spirit-led people invest in that Word.

## THE CLAIMS OF TRUTH

Essential to Warfield's understanding of Scripture is the confession that the Bible is an oracular book, that is to say, rather than merely being a word about God, the Bible is the very Word of God.[7] While truly coming to us through the words of human beings and evidencing the realities of human authorship, the Bible is nevertheless nothing less than "the crystallized voice of God."[8] The church

6. Moisés Silva, "Old Princeton, Westminster, and Inerrancy," in Johnson, *B. B. Warfield*, 77.

7. *I&A*, 106, 148, 318; see also *SSW*, 2:576.

8. *I&A*, 317; cf. 125, 147. As the Word of God, a revelation given by the Holy Spirit, the Bible enjoys "a Divine quality unattainable by human powers alone" (ibid., 131, 158). As such, the Bible is unique, dissimilar to all other literature.

"looks upon the Bible as an oracular book—as the Word of God in such a sense that whatever it says God says—not a book, then, in which one may, by searching, find some word of God, but a book which may be frankly appealed to at any point with assurance that whatever it may be found to say, that is the Word of God."[9] This was often summarized by Warfield by the formula "whatever Scripture says God says."[10]

The Bible is the Word of God because it is an inspired book. That the Bible is inspired entailed three affirmations for Hodge and Warfield. First, inspiration speaks of the *origin* of the text. It had become common among Warfield's more liberal contemporaries to speak of inspiration as either an effect upon the reader or a vague influence upon the human author. Indeed, we do use the word *inspired* in just these ways. We find a piece of music inspiring. And Michelangelo's David is an inspired work of sculpture. So that which is inspired either affects the subject in some way or is extraordinary in some manner that sets it off from the mundane. Neither of these notions, however, captures what Paul is saying in 2 Timothy 3:16 when he claims that all Scripture is given by inspiration. The Bible bears a quality that does not arise from the created order. Rather than finding its source and character from immanent effects or talents, the Scriptures are given by God (cf. 2 Peter 1:21). Paul uses the word *theopneustos*, meaning "God-breathed." Though often translated as "inspired," the idea would be better expressed as "expired." Paul is not saying that the Bible is inspired in the sense that God *breathes into* the text his imprimatur after the fact, but rather that Scripture is *breathed out* in that it comes from God. God is the speaker, the author. "The Scriptures are a divine product."[11]

9. *I&A*, 106.

10. *I&A*, 119, 420; *SSW*, 2:572; see also *Inspiration*, 29.

11. *I&A*, 133; cf. 275, 286–91. "When Paul declares, then, that 'every scripture', or 'all scripture' is the product of the Divine breath, 'is God-breathed', he asserts with as much energy as he could employ that Scripture is the product of a specifically Divine operation" (ibid; cf. 136, 151; *Inspiration*, 18ff.). The esv reading, "breathed out by God," is preferred over those translations that use the word *inspiration*.

The second entailment of the Bible as an inspired book is its *infallibility*. John Frame succinctly catches the idea here when he writes that "to breathe out words is to speak. To say that God breathes out errors is to say that he speaks errors. That is biblically impossible. God does not lie (Titus 1:2) and he does not make mistakes (Heb. 4:12). So he speaks only truth."[12] The truthfulness of the text, its inerrancy, is thus a natural implication of its being the speech of God. Scripture insists that God is a truth teller—he cannot lie—and he is ignorant of nothing.[13] Thus, being the breathed-out speech of God, the Bible is not only inerrant—without errors—but also infallible—incapable of error.[14]

The third natural entailment of the Bible as the oracles of God is its *divine authority*. Hodge and Warfield wrote that "the great design and effect of inspiration is to render the Sacred Scriptures in all their parts a divinely infallible and authoritative rule of faith and practice."[15] As the Word of God written, the Scriptures have an unimpeachable right to commend belief and agreement, and to demand obedience. God so associates himself with his Word that rejection of that Word is a rejection of its divine author. When Adam and Eve disobeyed God's spoken prohibition relative to the tree of the knowledge of good and evil, they alienated themselves from God. To disobey God's Word is to disobey *him*. To trust God's Word is to trust *him*. To hear the Word is to hear *him*.[16] "Thus (we

12. John M. Frame, *The Doctrine of the Word of God* (Phillipsburg, NJ: P&R Publishing, 2010), 547.

13. Num. 23:19; Pss. 19:9; 33:13–15; 119:160; John 17:17; Rom. 3:4; 2 Tim. 2:13; Titus 1:2; Heb. 4:12–13; 6:18. See *Inspiration*, 42; *I&A*, 131, 438.

14. See Frame, *Doctrine of the Word of God*, 169, for an interesting discussion on the relationship between inerrancy and infallibility. I am following his affirmation of a strong sense of infallibility. "I would say that Scripture is both inerrant and infallible. It is inerrant because it is infallible. There are no errors because there *can be* no errors in the divine speech."

15. *Inspiration*, 25.

16. Ibid., 29. While Warfield can sometimes seem ponderous to the modern reader, he was able to draw together the core of his understanding of the doctrine of inspiration into marvelously sharp and lucid paragraphs. For example, "Our Lord and his apostles looked upon the entire truthfulness and utter trustworthiness of that body

may say) God has *invested* himself in his words, or we could say that God has so *identified* himself with his words that whatever someone does to God's word (whether it is to obey or to disobey) they do directly to God himself."[17]

It is the divine authorship of Scripture—its unique inspiration by the Holy Spirit, its infallible truth, and its unimpeachable divine authority—that was under assault in Warfield's generation of theological scholarship. And defending the Bible as the Word of God was the primary goal of Warfield's apologetic efforts. But the very idea of the Bible as an inspired and authoritative Word of God is itself dependent upon an understanding of reality in which God is separate from the world, yet is able as he wills to reveal himself to the world. God can act in history and declare his redemptive love and will for his people. The God of biblical religion is a personal Creator. As such he jealously protects his right to act and speak, to engage in speech and action that must be acknowledged as his own and not be confused with the products of human religious imagination. Warfield unabashedly declares that "the religion of the Bible is frankly supernatural." Most fundamentally this means that "God has intervened extraordinarily, in the course of the sinful world's development, for the salvation of men otherwise lost."[18] Such intervention, Warfield insists, is the touchstone of biblical religion. The acts and words of God are not our projections but his revelation.

Warfield was concerned about the rising subjectivism in late nineteenth-century religious thought that confused God's revelation with human religious experience. The religious subject had become the object. Warfield found a common religious impulse in both the enthusiasm of popular religion and the rationalism of

---

of writings which they called 'Scripture', as so fully guaranteed by the inspiration of God, that they could appeal to them confidently in all their statements of whatever kind as absolutely true; adduce their deliverances on whatever subjects with a simple 'it is written', as the end of all strife; and treat them generally in a manner which clearly exhibits that in their view 'Scripture says' was equivalent to 'God says'." *SSW*, 2:580.

17. Ward, *Words of Life*, 27.

18. *I&A*, 71; cf. *Inspiration*, 24.

critical liberalism. Both mysticism and rationalism—as he called them—find the truth of religion within man rather than revealed from any point external to us. Each centers faith in the human self and in the end eradicates any distinction between the self and the divine.[19]

Warfield's entire apologetic enterprise was aimed at defending the objectivity of the Christian faith. God is a personal, transcendent Other. And his Word is his, coming *to* us, rather than from us. Given that Warfield's overt intention was to defend the Bible as an objective Word of God, his detractors have often accused him of objectivism. This is due, at least in part, to Warfield's own concerns about subjectivism. Thus he might very well have overloaded the objective a bit. He could have said more about the internal testimony of the Spirit when he spoke of the evidences for the Bible as the inspired Word of God. But the work of the Spirit was not under attack, only the idea that the Word is external to us. The objectivist charge is also the product of how the Princetonians sometimes spoke of theology as an objective science, the importance of the scientific method for theological inquiry, the Bible as a factual book, and the relationship between argument and proof. I believe that these features of nineteenth-century Princetonianism were simply conventional and not determinative for either Charles Hodge—who gets the lion share of criticism here—or B. B. Warfield.[20] The remark of Timothy Ward seems eminently fair:

19. Andrew W. Hoffecker, *Piety and the Princeton Theologians: Archibald Alexander, Charles Hodge, and Benjamin Warfield* (Phillipsburg, NJ: Presbyterian and Reformed, 1981), 124–27.

20. See John Vander Stelt, *Philosophy and Scripture: A Study of Old Princeton and Westminster Theology* (Marlburg, NJ: Mack Publishing, 1978), for an unrelenting attack upon Princeton centering on these sorts of concerns. Also see Jack Rogers and Donald McKim, *The Authority and Interpretation of the Bible* (San Francisco: Harper & Row, 1979), who argue the thesis that the Princetonian doctrine of Scripture was the product of an uncritical acceptance of Common Sense Realism. For a concerted rebuttal of the rationalist and Common Sense Realist criticisms, see Paul Kjoss Helseth, *"Right Reason" and the Princeton Mind: An Unorthodox Proposal* (Phillipsburg, NJ: P&R Publishing, 2010).

When a search is launched for those theologians or Christian groups who might have turned Scripture from being a living Word into a compendium of facts, the usual suspects rounded up and brought in for questioning are the 19th and 20th century theologians from Princeton Seminary, especially Warfield and Hodge. Indeed living as they did in an era in which scientific rationality loomed large as a criterion by which every claim of truth was to be tested, and affected as they inevitably were by the culture surrounding them, it is unsurprising that some of their statements and approaches to Scripture seem to be more interested in facts stated in Scripture than in God's dynamic action in and through Scripture.[21]

Warfield did emphasize the role of external evidences in his doctrine of Scripture more than he did the internal testimony of the Holy Spirit, but it cannot be said that his understanding of Scripture had no need of the Spirit. He stood firmly in the Calvinist and Westminster tradition. As such, his approach is fully in keeping with the Confession of Faith 1.5, which after enumerating a number of evidences for the self-authenticating nature of Scripture as the Word, adds the all-important statement:

> Yet notwithstanding, our full persuasion and assurance of the infallible truth and divine authority thereof, is from the inward work of the Holy Spirit bearing witness by and with the Word in our hearts.

In agreement with Westminster, Warfield declared:

> It lies more fundamentally still in the postulate that these Scriptures are accredited to us as the revelation of God solely by the testimony of the Holy Spirit—that without this testimony they lie before us inert and without effect on our hearts and minds, while with it they become not merely the power of God

21. Ward, *Words of Life*, 134.

unto salvation, but also the vitalizing source of our knowledge of God.[22]

The work of the Spirit is absolutely essential to any consideration of the Word of God, both in generating that Word in the first place, and in our apprehension and response to it. Faith is not the result of a human work or disposition, but is a supernatural gift of God. But the Spirit does not work an irrational or groundless faith in us. Warfield rejects any fideistic notion of faith. Drawing much of this together in an essay on the doctrine of Scripture in the Confession of Faith, Warfield wrote:

> According to the Confession, then, as according to the whole of Reformed theology, man needs something else than evidence fully to persuade him to believe and obey God's Word—he needs the work of the Holy Spirit accompanying the Word, *ab extra incidens*. This is but to say that faith in God's Word is not man's own work, but the gift of God, and that man needs a preparation of the spirit as well as an exhibition of the evidences in order to yield faith and obedience.[23]

The Calvinist principle of the correlation of the Spirit and the Word "is at the heart of the Princeton epistemology."[24] Objective arguments, evidences, exist in abundance for the divinity of Scripture, yet despite their cogency and inherent rational integrity, they are incapable of producing saving faith. That is the sovereign work of the Spirit. Yet the Spirit does not work apart from the Word. Like the Hodges before him, Warfield

> always emphasized that, ultimately, commitment to biblical authority came only by the special work of the sovereign Holy

22. B. B. Warfield, *Calvin and Augustine*, ed. Samuel G. Craig (Philadelphia: Presbyterian and Reformed, 1956), 115.
23. *SSW*, 2:567.
24. Hoffecker, *Piety and the Princeton Theologians*, 104.

Spirit. Evidence can show that the Bible is trustworthy, but evidence alone can never be sufficient to bring conviction to our souls that it is the Word of God or bring submission to its authority. Only the testimony of the Holy Spirit can accomplish this.[25]

Christian faith is always subjective, for it is the dependence of the human subject upon Christ. Andrew Hoffecker argues that similar to Friedrich Schleiermacher, "Warfield is perfectly content with the notion of religion as dependence." But for Warfield, religion is groundless and subjectivistic if it is not "dependence on a specific object, i.e., God."[26] Warfield will have neither objectivism nor subjectivism. "Our knowledge of God is covenantal." It is our knowing, but our knowing is always a response to God's objective revelation of himself.[27] In light of the rise of higher critical forces after the Civil War, Warfield was certainly given to emphasize the external evidences for the inspiration and authority of Scripture, yet he also acknowledged the necessity of the Spirit for our subjective appropriation of the text. "Neither the objective side (the biblical text itself) nor the subjective side (the Spirit's inward witness) can function without the other."[28]

## THE CHURCH: A PILLAR OF TRUTH

### The "Church-Doctrine" of Inspiration

It was common for Warfield to begin essays on the doctrine of Scripture by approaching the topic from the perspective of faith. Over and over again, he wrote of the "church-doctrine" of inspiration, by which he meant the catholic belief, held by the church from the time of apostles, that the Bible is the inspired, reliable, and authoritative

25. Cannata, "Warfield and the Doctrine of Scripture," 103.

26. Hoffecker, *Piety and the Princeton Theologians*, 143.

27. Frame, *Doctrine of the Word of God*, 542.

28. Ibid., 527. Frame is speaking explicitly of Cornelius Van Til here, but the comment holds for Warfield as well.

Word of God.[29] Warfield calls this the church-doctrine of inspiration because it arises spontaneously from the Spirit-led "instinct" of the people of God as their natural, covenantal response to the Word.[30]

To be sure, Warfield's church-doctrine construct is meant to function polemically, as one can see when he writes, "Over against the numberless discordant theories of inspiration which vex our time, there stands a well-defined church-doctrine of inspiration."[31] Yet there is something far more constructive than an argument about historical pride of place going on here. Warfield commends the church's historic belief in the Bible as the proper starting point for our reflections relative to the doctrine of Scripture. While faith in Christ is worked upon the heart by the internal testimony of the Spirit, belief also comes to us in a community of persons. The life and faith of the church are the natural heritage of all who know Jesus as Lord and Savior. And a crucial element of that life has always been a trust in the truthfulness of the Word of God.[32] The instinctive conviction that the Bible is an infallible rule of faith is as natural to the people of God as is belief in Christ.

Of course, the church's constant and abiding conviction that the Bible is a God-breathed, infallible guide to faith and life would be nothing more than human opinion if it did not conform to an objective reality. The integrity of any article of faith is dependent upon the integrity of its object. If the Bible were not the Word of God all the belief in the world that it is would not make it so. Warfield's

29. *Inspiration*, 18, 23, 26, 32, 34. The substance of Warfield's "church-doctrine" infuses the work he wrote with A. A. Hodge, yet the phrase itself seems to be Warfield's own.

30. *I&A*, 106–7: "This attitude of entire trust in every word of the Scriptures has been characteristic of the people of God from the very foundation of the church. Christendom has always reposed upon the belief that the utterances of this book are properly oracles of God. The whole body of Christian literature bears witness to this fact. We may trace its stream to its source, and everywhere it is vocal with a living faith in the divine trustworthiness of the Scriptures of God."

31. *I&A*, 106.

32. Notice, for example, how Warfield begins his 1909 essay "Inspiration" by saying that "From the very beginning, and unbroken since," the church-doctrine of inspiration "has been distinctly the vital belief of the Christian people." *SSW*, 2:618–21.

response here is that our confidence in the Bible as God's Word is but the proper subjective complement to what Scripture says about itself and shows itself to be. The variety and pervasiveness of the Bible's witness to its own oracular nature and credibility as a truthful testimony in all it says suggests that "the church-doctrine of inspiration is simply a transcript of the biblical doctrine."[33] Indeed, the "church-doctrine of inspiration was the Bible doctrine before it was the church-doctrine, and is the church-doctrine only because it was the Bible doctrine."[34] What the people of God have always and everywhere believed about the Bible, that it is his breathed-out Word, is not an expression of a subjectivist preference, but rather is a Spirit-led, instinctive response to the written Word of God.

## A Trustworthy Word

Though the phrase *the inerrancy of the Bible* is justifiably linked with the name of Warfield, the truth is Warfield himself did not

33. *I&A*, 120.

34. Ibid., 114; cf. 422. Perhaps no single paragraph of Warfield's corpus is as closely packed relative to the topic under discussion as is this one from ibid., 173–74 ("The Real Problem of Inspiration"): "The Church, then, has held from the beginning that the Bible is the Word of God in such a sense that its words though written by men and bearing indelibly impressed upon them the marks of their human origin, were written, nevertheless, under such an influence of the Holy Ghost as to be also the words of God, the adequate expression of His mind and will. It has always recognized that this conception of co-authorship implies that the Spirit's superintendence extends to the choice of the words by the human authors (verbal inspiration), and preserves its product from everything inconsistent with a divine authorship—thus securing, among other things, that entire truthfulness which is everywhere presupposed in and asserted for Scripture by the Biblical writers (inerrancy). Whatever minor variations may now and again have entered into the mode of statement, this has always been the core of the Church doctrine of inspiration. And along with many other modes of commending and defending it, the primary ground on which it has been held by the Church as the true doctrine is that it is the Biblical authors themselves, and has therefore the whole mass of evidence for it which goes to show that the Biblical writers are trustworthy as doctrinal guides. It is the testimony of the Bible itself to its own origin and character as the Oracles of the Most High, that has led the Church to her acceptance of it as such, and to her dependence on it not only for her doctrine of Scripture, but for the whole body of her doctrinal teaching, which is looked upon by her as divine because drawn from this divinely given fountain of truth."

much like the term.[35] *Inerrancy* and its cognates appear repeatedly in Hodge and Warfield's *Inspiration*, but are surprisingly rare in Warfield's later independent work.[36] Already by Warfield's time, a good bit of the discussion had devolved into a debate about the propriety of the word *inerrancy*, and he would spend no small amount of effort defending the doctrine—and the term—from misunderstandings and misuse. Yet Warfield did affirm that the word *inerrancy*, however inelegant and clumsy it might be, does sharply affirm the absolute truthfulness of God's Word. And for Warfield, that is what *inerrancy* means: "the entire truthfulness of the Scriptures as given by God."

Far more common than "inerrant" in Warfield's corpus is the word *trustworthy*.[37] Now, the word *trustworthy* might seem like a rather soft word to use in describing the truthfulness of the Bible. After all, the word could convey no more than the notion of general

35. David Calhoun notes that while Warfield fervently affirmed the substance of the doctrine of biblical inerrancy, he wrote that "the phrase 'the inerrancy of the original autographs' [was] not an altogether happy one to express the doctrine of the Scriptures and of the Westminster Confession as to the entire truthfulness of the Scriptures as given by God." David B. Calhoun, *Princeton Seminary*, 2 vols. (Edinburgh: Banner of Truth, 1996), 2:142. See *SSW*, 2:582.

36. The greater portion of inerrancy language (e.g., "without error") appears in Hodge's section of the work. See *Inspiration*, 9–10, 17, 26–28, 30, 35, 38.

37. For example, after bemoaning the fact that the word *inerrancy* has become a "bone of contention," and that the issue before the church in light of the rise of destructive biblical criticism is "more vital than the bare 'inerrancy' of the Scriptures," Warfield claims that the real issue is that of "the trustworthiness of the Bible in its express declarations, and in the fundamental conceptions of its writers as to the course of the history of God's dealings with his people. It concerns, in a word, the authority of the Biblical representations concerning the nature of revealed religion, and the mode and course of its revelation. The issue raised is whether we are to look upon the Bible as containing a divinely guaranteed and wholly trustworthy account of God's redemptive revelation, and the course of his gracious dealings with his people; or as merely a mass of more or less trustworthy materials, out of which we are to sift the fact in order to put together a trustworthy account of God's redemptive revelation and the course of his dealings with his people." *SSW*, 2:581–82. Obviously, the word *trustworthy* cannot stand alone, as Warfield himself qualifies it here to be used in two senses, or at least in two degrees. When Warfield does not qualify the word, as he does when he says "more or less trustworthy," he means fully trustworthy, completely trustworthy, even divinely trustworthy.

reliability. But when it is read in light of Warfield's affirmation of Scripture as the objectively given, divinely inspired Word of God, the *trustworthy* attributive takes on the strong sense of "absolutely reliable," "divinely reliable." Reliable in what? In everything it intends, and that includes its truth claims.

The word *trustworthy* has the advantage not only of attributing a characteristic to its object, but also of indicating the illocutionary effect or intention of the object. That which is trustworthy is worthy of trust. What a marvelously covenantal word. God's Word is inherently trustworthy because it is his Word and he is true in all things, and as such it elicits a "simple and robust trust in its every declaration." The inherent, objective trustworthiness of God's Word "imposes on us the duty of accepting" it as the truth of God.[38]

I am not by any means suggesting that the word *trustworthy* should replace *inerrant* as our fundamental descriptor for the truth of Scripture. *Trustworthy* is just too underdetermined in English denotation to carry the weight of objective truthfulness. *Inerrant* will have to do. But we should not miss the power of Warfield's recurrent use of the language of trustworthiness, and perhaps a comparative limitation of the term *inerrant*. While it is important to say that the Bible is without error, fully truthful in all it asserts, that is not enough. "Presumably a good dictionary is error-free, but that does not raise its status above that of just a dictionary."[39] The Bible is more than merely a truth-telling piece of literature. Its Spirit-inspired truth compels a reverence and trust, an "entire subjection to every declaration." Warfield helps us see just what is at stake in the entire inerrancy discussion, and why it inherently entails a covenantally responsive element, when he addresses it to real-world pastoral contexts:

> As we sit in the midst of our pupils in the Sabbath-school, or in the centre of our circle at home, or perchance at some bedside of

38. *I&A*, 142, 213.
39. Ward, *Words of Life*, 136.

sickness or of death; or as we meet our fellow-man amid the busy work of the world, hemmed in by temptation or weighed down with care, and would fain put beneath him some firm support and stay: in what spirit do we turn to this Bible then? With what confidence do we commend its every word to those whom we would make partakers of its comfort or of its strength? In such scenes as these is revealed the vital faith of the people of God in the surety and trustworthiness of the Word of God.[40]

## The Presumption of Truth

Because the focal point of Warfield's doctrine of Scripture was his opposition to the inroads of modern theology and its dependence upon the higher critical method, we should not be surprised that his engagement with higher criticism sheds light upon his heavy use of trust language.[41] Nineteenth-century critical study of the Bible emphasized the human character of the biblical texts, and for that Warfield was grateful. Failure to recognize or accredit the human authorship of Scripture ends in a docetic view of the text and a dictational conception of its production.[42] If the church has

40. *I&A*, 107. These sorts of comments in Warfield make it somewhat surprising that his conception of inerrancy has sometimes been described as merely an oracular construct. While placing some of the responsibility upon those who came after Warfield, Anthony Thiselton suggests that Warfield tended toward a model of revelation that was unduly impersonal and oriented to the distribution of information and thus did not give sufficient attention to the force or effect of Scripture. It is certainly true that Warfield did describe the Bible variously as "sacred teaching" and "the adequate expression of His mind and will," and expended much of his energies in the defense of the Bible as the objective truth of God. Yet Thiselton's evaluation of Warfield does not demonstrate a generous reading. Anthony Thiselton, "Authority and Hermeneutics: Some Proposals for a More Creative Agenda," in *A Pathway into the Holy Scripture*, ed. Philip Satterthwaite and David F. Wright (Grand Rapids: Eerdmans, 1994), 110–15. The same sorts of criticisms appear in Kevin Vanhoozer's contribution to the same volume ("God's Mighty Speech-Acts: The Doctrine of Scripture Today," 151, 163).

41. "The Princeton formulations of inerrancy were meant precisely to counteract the growing popularity of nineteenth-century critical theories." Silva, "Old Princeton, Westminster, and Inerrancy," 88.

42. *SSW*, 2:542–45.

sometimes been guilty of marginalizing the human authorship and thus the true humanity of the Bible, modern critical studies have fallen into the opposite fault of thinking "that it was man and man alone who made the Bible; and that it is, therefore, a purely human book." While admitting that some liberal scholars did entertain understandings of inspiration that allowed for divine influence of the biblical authors, Warfield was more likely to typify the debate in simple either-or terms. Either the Bible was written by human beings under the inspiration of the Holy Spirit,[43] or the Bible was the product of a human enterprise in which divine influence was either insignificant or dismissed. Either the Bible is inspired, and hence is the very Word of God, or it is not inspired, and is not God's Word.[44] Given that modern critical scholarship holds that the Bible is the product of human religious experience alone, and like all records of human experience is to be evaluated solely within a naturalistic framework, "there is no standing ground between the two theories of full verbal inspiration and no inspiration at all."[45]

Warfield was convinced that the critical opposition to the inspiration of the Bible has its roots not in some evidence that the Bible is not inspired but in a denial of the doctrine based upon an ideology of critical doubt. The forest of critical theories and proposals are so confusing that "wherever five 'advanced thinkers' assemble, at

43. A. N. S. Lane writes that "throughout his writings as a whole Warfield stresses the divine authorship of scripture far more than the human." A. N. S. Lane, "B. B. Warfield on the Humanity of Scripture," *VE* 16 (1986): 78. While certainly true, one would be hard-pressed to find a single Warfield treatise on the doctrine of Scripture in which he does not reference the doctrine of *concursus*: "The Scriptures are merely the product of Divine and human forces working together to produce a product in the production of which the human forces work under the initiation and prevalent direction of the Divine." *I&A*, 162; cf. *Inspiration*, 71; *I&A*, 83, 92–3, 125, 153, 155, 158, 160, 173, 421–22; *SSW*, 2:546–47, 629, 631.

44. Warfield held that "the new critical theories are consciously inconsistent with the old doctrine of inspiration" and that "it is clear that one or the other must go to the wall." *SSW*, 1:131–32. Lesslie Newbigin, *Proper Confidence: Faith, Doubt and Certainty in Christian Discipleship* (Grand Rapids: Eerdmans, 1995), 101, notes that liberal scholars typically reject any depiction of the Bible as the Word of God.

45. *I&A*, 441.

least six theories as to inspiration are likely to be ventilated." While each disagrees with the others, they all agree that "there is less of the truth of God and more of the error of man in the Bible than Christians have wont to believe. . . . They agree only in their common destructive attitude towards some higher view of the inspiration of the Bible."[46]

The higher critical method presupposed Rene Descartes' principle of methodological doubt. All assertions must be doubted, even assumed to be false, until they are proved true by the light of critical reason. Applied to the Bible, methodological doubt "created a prejudice in favor of doubt over truth."[47] As the Enlightenment placed human reason in an adversarial relationship to the rest of creation, so the principle of methodological doubt adopts a hostile attitude toward the Bible. This negative attitude parades as a concern for scientific integrity, but is actually a religious prejudice against the Word of God, for it is now false until it is proved true by Enlightenment canons of reason.

Trust, taking God at his Word, submitting to his truth, is the exact opposite of doubt. If methodological doubt represents a prejudice against the truthfulness of the Bible, the instinct of the people of God is to believe the inspired Word and to trust its divine author. Rather than working from a presumption of error and demanding that every assertion be rationally proved before it can be accepted, the regenerate come to Scripture with a predisposition that it is true. This is thoroughly Augustinian—"I believe in order to understand"—but not fideistic. The predisposition of trust is "legitimate" and "sound"[48] because the Bible claims and shows itself to be a God-breathed Word. The proper response, the covenantal complement of the objectively given Word of God is the complete trust of God's people in his Word. We approach the Scriptures "with the very strong presumption that all these Scrip-

---

46. Ibid., 105; cf. *SSW*, 2:581.
47. Newbigin, *Proper Confidence*, 24.
48. *Inspiration*, 34; *I&A*, 121–23.

tures contain no errors," with the expectation that "the Bible is the Word of God, every detail of the meaning of which is of inestimable preciousness."[49]

It is unfortunate that the criticism of Scripture has been used as "an engine to undermine the divine authority of Scripture" and thus shake the confidence of believers in God's Word. Though the higher criticism that is presently in vogue presupposes a naturalistic and historicist worldview, historical criticism is not to be rejected. "Far from the Bible being less subject to criticism than other books," Warfield wrote, "we are bound to submit [the Bible's] unique claims to a criticism of unique rigor. Criticism is the mode of procedure by which we assure ourselves that it is what it claims to be."[50] In other words, Warfield refuses to allow the doctrine of inspiration to become an occasion for obscurantism, a refusal to investigate the phenomena of the text on theological grounds. To say that the Bible is inerrant because it is the inspired Word of God, and that God cannot lie, and then leave it at that, refusing to look closely at the Bible's own claims of truth, betrays a certain intellectual cowardice and a confessional insecurity. Rather, the very doctrine of the divine authorship and authority of Scripture is an invitation to investigate the phenomena, to take the text and its claims with absolute seriousness. "By all means," Warfield insists, "let the doctrine of the Bible be tested by the facts and let the test be made all the more, not the less, stringent and penetrating because of the great issues that hang upon it."[51]

Warfield's comments regarding what he calls the "rights of criticism" are extremely strong. But he is no less insistent regarding the appropriate disposition under which historical criticism is to take place. And here again we see his concern for the subjective, heart attitude of the people of God as they come to God's Word. The study of the phenomena of Scripture is not to be neglected, but it is

49. *I&A*, 215, 110; cf. 438.
50. *SSW*, 2:595.
51. *I&A*, 217.

to be pursued with great care. We come to it with a predisposition toward the truthfulness of the Bible.[52] This is God's authoritative Word. We must come to it "with infinite humility and teachableness, and with prayer for the constant guidance of the gracious Spirit."[53]

This presumption of truth as the proper complement to the divinely inspired Word is so strong that it places the burden of proof upon those who would seek to deny the truthfulness of Scripture. While Warfield can say that "no error can be proved to exist within the sacred pages," and that "modern criticism has absolutely no valid argument to bring against the church doctrine of verbal inspiration, drawn from the phenomena of Scripture,"[54] he realizes that he is speaking as much from his confessional stance as he is from the probabilistic results of evidential argument. As public truth, a declaration about the real character of God's world and human historical existence in the world, the biblical testimony to reality is never shut off from the possibility of critical investigation. Indeed, Warfield invites it. But such investigation, if it is intended to undermine the divine authorship or truthfulness of Scripture, must demonstrate indubitably that either the Bible's claims about its own inspiration are patently false or that the Bible possesses unresolvable contradictions or traffics in palpable errors. Any such falsehoods or errors must be established beyond doubt in order to overturn the historic presumption of the people of God that God is true to his Word.[55]

Even the most careful and faithful historical criticism cannot prove every truth-claim of Scripture. Our present knowledge of history and science are such that we see any number of difficulties when we seek to harmonize the Bible with these disciplines. It is simply fallacious to think that we must be able to account for all the contents before we subject ourselves to its divine authority. As

52. Ibid., 214.
53. *Inspiration*, 35; cf. 39.
54. *I&A*, 440.
55. *Inspiration*, 34–42, 54; *I&A*, 226, 423.

John Frame writes: "We confess the Bible as the Word of God not because we have solved all the difficulties, but because God himself (in the text) and the Spirit (in our hearts) has so identified it."[56] While the force of the evidence for the trustworthiness of Scripture is compelling to the regenerate heart, and that evidence makes our confidence in the truthfulness of the Word a sound and rational act, we will never prove every Bible claim of truth. Indeed, many stand beyond any kind of historical criticism. Warfield cites the biblical testimony to the triune nature of God and the incarnation of Christ as examples.[57] Sinclair Ferguson effectively captures the idea when he writes:

> We cannot prove that "Christ died for our sin according to the Scriptures" (1 Cor. 15:3) is an infallible statement. We do affirm that such a statement is coherent within itself, the rest of Scripture, and the universe in which we live. We subscribe to biblical authority not on the grounds of our ability to prove it but because of the persuasiveness of its testimony to be God's own Word.[58]

Thus, the burden is not ours to prove that all of Scripture is true; it belongs rather, to those who believe it is not to prove any of it otherwise.

## Investment in Truth

Warfield's doctrine of the inspiration of Scripture assumes and affirms that the Bible is a divine gift, a means of grace to sinful human beings.[59] There is no other way to account for, make sense of, or appreciate the existence of the Bible than as the absolutely unique redemptive voice of God. Further, this revelation is not given to the world haphazardly or generically. God's speech is a

56. Frame, *Doctrine of the Word of God*, 544.

57. *I&A*, 215.

58. Sinclair Ferguson, "How Does the Bible Look at Itself?" in *Inerrancy and Hermeneutic*, ed. Harvie Conn (Grand Rapids: Baker, 1988), 64.

59. E.g., *I&A*, 72, 95, 100, 154, 213; *SSW*, 2:588.

personal and intentional communication, and as such it assumes an audience. For Warfield, this is essential to the distinction between general and special revelation. God's general revelation is by its very nature accessible to all human beings. His special revelation, his redemptive Word, is intended for "the creation in men of the gracious God, forming a people for Himself, that they may show forth his praise." In other words, this redemptive revelation is given "to a special class of sinners, to whom God would make known His salvation."[60] The Bible is God's Word to God's people. It is, as Ferguson has said, "the canon of God's people's lives."[61] Warfield drew this same conclusion from his reading of such texts as Romans 15:4; 4:23–24 and 2 Timothy 3:16–17. Do not leave out verse 17: "that the man of God may be competent, equipped for every good work."

The church has a stake in the doctrine of the inspiration of Scripture as the church bears a ministerial responsibility to the Word. Francis Turretin enumerated five such ministries:[62] (1) the church is the keeper and preserver of the oracles of God; (2) the church is the guide who points people to the Word; (3) the church is the defender of the Bible, guarding that which is genuinely canonical and separating it from the spurious ("in which sense she may be called the ground [hedraioma] of the truth [1 Tim. 3:15]"); (4) the church is the herald who proclaims the truth of Scripture; and, (5) the church is the interpreter of the Scripture, that body vouchsafed with unfolding the true sense of the text.[63] Turretin is quick to point out that the church's responsibilities relative to Scripture in no way imply a magisterial role for the church. "Through her, indeed, we believe, but not on account of her." Yet there is a close association in the Reformed mind, and certainly in Warfield's, between the Holy Spirit, the Word, and the church. The Spirit uses the church's ministry of the Word to bring sinners to faith. The church's faithful

60. *I&A*, 72–74.

61. Ferguson, "How Does the Bible Look at Itself?" 63.

62. Francis Turretin, *Institutes of Elenctic Theology*, ed. James T. Dennison, trans. George Musgrave Giger, 3 vols. (Phillipsburg, NJ: P&R Publishing, 1992), 1:90.

63. Cf. *I&A*, 106, 128.

handling and proclamation of the redemptive Word is the instrument by which the Spirit works.[64]

Warfield was adamant that the authority of Scripture rests with God and not the church, that "the Church does not 'determine' the Scriptures, but the Scriptures the Church."[65] Indeed, the Word imposes a series of tasks or callings upon the church. We might even say that the Bible impresses an identity upon the church. We are the people who keep and defend, interpret and study, proclaim and teach the Word (Turretin's ministries). These are not just tasks we engage in; they are kingdom-related callings that shape us and make us who we are.

We are both dependent upon and responsible to the Word as the people of God who are drawn into the redemptive action of Scripture. We are dependent upon Scripture as we owe all that we are as the body of Christ to its revelatory and redemptive power. Thus Warfield writes:

> Let it suffice to say that to a plenarily inspired Bible, humbly trusted as such, we actually, and as a matter of fact, owe all that has blessed our lives with hopes of an immortality of bliss, and with the present fruition of the love of God in Christ. . . . It is actually to the Bible that you and I owe it that we have a Christ—a Christ to love, to trust and to follow, a Christ without us the ground of our salvation, a Christ within us the hope of glory.[66]

64. Ward, *Words of Life*, 152, summarizes the point nicely: "If the question is why, or on account of what, do I believe the Bible to be divine, I will answer that I do so on account of the Scripture itself which by its marks proves itself to be such. If it is asked whence or from what I believe, I will answer from the Holy Spirit, who produces that belief in me. Finally, if I am asked by what means or instrument I believe it, I will answer through the church which God uses in delivering the Scriptures to me."

65. *SSW*, 2:538. Over against the Roman Catholic doctrine of the magisterial role of the church over Scripture, James Packer has wonderfully commented that "the Church no more gave us the New Testament canon than Sir Isaac Newton gave us the force of gravity." J. I. Packer, *God Speaks to Man: Revelation and the Bible*, Christian Foundations 6 (Philadelphia: Westminster, 1965), 81.

66. *I&A*, 126–27; cf. 187: "We have no Christ except the one whom the apostles have given to us."

We are to receive the Word of God with the same reverence we owe to Jesus, for as Calvin wrote "We receive him as he is offered by the Father: namely, clothed with his gospel."[67] Everything we are is invested in the trustworthiness of Scripture as a sure guide to our life as the people God. What we value and hold dear, how we see the world and lean into it, the choices we have made in our lives, our hopes for the future—tomorrow and eternally—are tied up in the trust we invest in God's Word. This is how we approach the Word, for this is who we are. "We know how," Warfield wrote, "as Christian men, we approach this Holy Book—how unquestionably we receive its statements of fact, bow before its enunciations of duty, tremble before its threatenings, and rest upon its promises."[68]

With joy and zeal we enter into the biblical story, know its past as our own covenantal memory, live in its ways, and pursue its mission as the highest possible calling of redeemed human beings. The Bible is God's Word. But it might be better to call it God's Word to God's people. By the power of God's Spirit, his divinely inspired and utterly infallible Word calls forth a people who trust him body and soul, in life and in death. The Bible is authoritative because it is God's own breath. But its lived authority is covenantal. As God's Word to his people, it demands the response of our absolute trust. Calvin caught it just so: "The Scriptures obtain full authority among believers only when men regard them as having sprung from heaven, as if there the living words of God were heard."[69]

The covenantal payout of Warfield's construction of the doctrine of the inspiration of Scripture is that the people of God can never be cool or dispassionate toward the Bible and its truth. We are predisposed toward its truth. We come to it expecting God to speak truth. When we say that the Bible is the inerrant word of God, we mean both that the Bible is completely true in all it affirms and that

67. John Calvin, *Institutes of the Christian Religion*, ed. John T. McNeill, trans. Ford Lewis Battles, 2 vols. (Philadelphia: Westminster, 1975), 3.2.6.
68. *I&A*, 106.
69. Calvin, *Institutes*, 1.7.1.

we approach it as the very Word of God. Our confession concerning the divine origin and authority of Scripture is as much about us as it is about the truth teller himself and his truth. Our instinctive conviction is that the Bible is an infallibly true guide to Christian faith and life. "The Christian man requires, and, thank God, has, a thoroughly trustworthy Bible to which he can go directly and at once in every time of need."[70] This very presumption of the Bible's truth means that we know ourselves as subject to its instruction, that we handle it with the utmost care, seeking to be responsible readers[71] of its treasures, and that we live out its story as a people of the Word as we look toward the appearing of our Savior.

---

70. *I&A*, 122.

71. The relationship between the inspiration of Scripture and hermeneutics is crucial to the issues of this chapter. Unfortunately, space has not allowed the pursuit of that discussion. Suffice it here to say that Hodge and Warfield clearly saw the connection and provide us with numerous critical insights in their *Inspiration*, e.g., 28, 31, 42–43, 62–63, 70–71. Also see Thiselton, "Authority and Hermeneutics," 113–22; Frame, *Doctrine of the Word of God*, 168–73; and Silva, "Old Princeton, Westminster, and Inerrancy," 80–89. On this connection, Silva quite rightly goes so far as to say that "for inerrancy to function properly in our use of Scripture, an adequate hermeneutics is a prerequisite. But that is a far cry from suggesting that the doctrine of inerrancy automatically provides us with the correct hermeneutics, except in the rather general sense that it precludes any interpretation that makes out God to lie or to err" (84).

# 3

# Deconstructing Canon: Recent Challenges to the Origins and Authority of the New Testament Writings

## MICHAEL J. KRUGER

KURT ALAND, IN HIS WELL-KNOWN work *The Problem of the New Testament Canon*, made the bold declaration that the "question of Canon will make its ways to the centre of the theological and ecclesiastical debate" because "the question is one which confronts not only the New Testament scholar, but every Christian theologian."[1] Aland's point is a profoundly simple one: the existence of the canon of Scripture raises such complex and profound questions about biblical authority that the impact is felt not only in the academy but also in the church. These questions are well known

1. Kurt Aland, *The Problem of the New Testament Canon* (London: A. R. Mowbray & Co., 1962), 31.

49

to all who study the canon.[2] Why is the New Testament canon limited to these twenty-seven books? What do all these books share in common? What was the process by which they were brought together? Why should the results of that process be normative for the modern church? What are we to make of disputes in the early church over these books? What of the abundance of apocryphal literature that has been discovered? And what would we do if we discovered a lost epistle of the apostle Paul? It is precisely these sorts of questions, and the complex issues they raise, that have led many to consider the problem of canon to be, as Ridderbos has observed, the "hidden, dragging, illness of the church."[3]

Of course, the problems associated with canon have not been missed by critics of biblical Christianity. Indeed, Aland's prediction has proved true in recent years as canonical questions not only continue to dominate the attention of biblical scholars, but have now made their way to the average person in the pew. A number of scholars have redirected their attentions away from the academy and placed them purely on the layman. Bart Ehrman has repeatedly focused upon canon issues in a number of popular-level books over the last decade, including *Lost Christianities, Misquoting Jesus, Jesus Interrupted*, and, most recently, *Forged*.[4] Elaine Pagels, who has also written extensively on canon issues over the years,[5] also has shifted her attention to popular-level books such as *Beyond Belief: The Secret*

2. For a full-length work on canon from a Reformed perspective, see my forthcoming *Canon Revisited: Establishing the Origins and Authority of the New Testament Books* (Wheaton, IL: Crossway, 2012).

3. Herman Ridderbos, "The Canon of the New Testament," in *Revelation and the Bible: Contemporary Evangelical Thought*, ed. Carl F. H. Henry (Grand Rapids: Baker, 1958), 198.

4. Bart D. Ehrman, *Lost Christianities: The Battles for Scripture and the Faiths We Never Knew* (New York: Oxford University Press, 2002); idem, *Misquoting Jesus: The Story behind Who Changed the Bible and Why* (San Francisco: HarperCollins, 2005); idem, *Jesus, Interrupted: Revealing the Hidden Contradictions in the Bible (and Why We Don't Know about Them)* (San Francisco: HarperOne, 2009); and idem, *Forged: Writing in the Name of God—Why the Bible's Authors Are Not Who We Think They Are* (New York: HarperOne, 2011).

5. E.g., Elaine Pagels, *The Gnostic Gospels* (New York: Random House, 1979).

*Gospel of Thomas*, in which she argues that Thomas was one of the earliest Gospels, even preceding the Gospel of John.[6] Lay-level interest in canonical issues has also been generated by recent archaeological discoveries, such as the Gospel of Judas, which continue to raise questions about whether there are other lost stories of Jesus just waiting to be discovered.[7] Such discoveries are often marketed to popular audiences through provocative titles such as *The Five Gospels*,[8] *Secrets from the Lost Gospel*,[9] and *Forgotten Scriptures*.[10] This shift in focus from the academy to the church (or to the public at large) is precisely why we must address this question afresh, as members of our own congregations are reading these books and asking these kinds of questions.

What are the precise arguments being used by critics of the canon today? What are their specific claims about the history of the canon and the way it developed? And how do these claims serve to undermine the traditional Christian approach to the canon? Within scholarship today, there are five major theses that form the backbone of the critical approach to the New Testament canon. These five theses are so entrenched within the modern academy (and so frequently repeated) that scholars often feel no need to make arguments for them—they are not so much the conclusion of the critical approach as they are its philosophical starting point. And it is these five theses that constitute the most formidable challenges to the traditional Christian approach to the canon. We shall explore

6. Elaine Pagels, *Beyond Belief: The Secret Gospel of Thomas* (New York: Random House, 2003).

7. James M. Robinson, *The Secrets of Judas: The Story of the Misunderstood Disciple and His Lost Gospel* (San Francisco: HarperSanFrancisco, 2006); Herbert Krosney, *The Lost Gospel: The Quest for the Gospel of Judas Iscariot* (Hanover, PA: National Geographic Society, 2006).

8. Robert W. Funk, *The Five Gospels: What Did Jesus Really Say?* (New York: Polebridge, 1993).

9. Kenneth Hanson, *Secrets from the Lost Bible: Hidden Scriptures Found* (Vancouver: Council Oak Books, 2004).

10. Lee Martin McDonald, *Forgotten Scriptures: The Selection and Rejection of Early Religious Writings* (Louisville: Westminster John Knox, 2009).

these theses one by one, offering an assessment of and response to each. Due to space limitations, we will need to restrict our discussion here to just the New Testament canon. But as we shall see, many of the points made about the New Testament canon will also have applicability to the challenges faced by the Old Testament canon.[11]

## Thesis #1: There Was Not a New Testament "Canon" until the Fourth Century

At the core of the critical approach to the New Testament canon is the claim that there was no New Testament "canon" prior to the fourth century. The literary situation prior to this period, we are told, was a loose and wide-open affair—early Christians read a "boundless, living mass of heterogenous"[12] texts, many of which were apocryphal in nature. It was not until the fourth century that any sort of meaningful limitation and restriction took place and thus it is only at this point that we can say that we have a New Testament "canon." Geoffrey Hahneman is typical in this regard: "The idea of a New Testament canon does not appear applicable before the fourth century."[13] Similarly, Albert Sundberg argues, "This interest [in the New Testament canon] first appears in our extant literature in Eusebius and Jerome . . . moving the decisive period of canonical history from the second century to the end of the second century onward into the fourth and beginning of the fifth century."[14] David Dungan, in his book *Constantine's Bible*, is most direct: "The creation of a canon of scripture was a unique

11. For more on the Old Testament canon, see Roger T. Beckwith, *The Old Testament Canon of the New Testament Church and Its Background in Early Judaism* (Grand Rapids: Eerdmans, 1986); and Andrew E. Steinmann, *The Oracles of God: The Old Testament Canon* (St. Louis: Concordia Academic Press, 1999).

12. David L. Dungan, *Constantine's Bible: Politics and the Making of the New Testament* (Philadelphia: Fortress Press, 2006), 132–33.

13. Geoffrey M. Hahneman, *The Muratorian Fragment and the Development of the Canon* (Oxford: Clarendon, 1992), 129–30.

14. Albert C. Sundberg, "Towards a Revised History of the New Testament Canon," *SE* 4 (1968): 460–61.

development . . . found for the first time in fourth- and fifth-century Romanized Catholic Christianity."[15]

Now, before offering a response to this first claim, it should be noted that there is an element of truth in it. Indeed, a full consensus on the canon was not finally reached until the fourth or fifth century, and, prior to this period, the borders of the canon were fuzzy at certain points. There were disagreements over canonical books—some early Christian communities received certain books as Scripture whereas others did not. Nevertheless, the general claim that the canon did not come about until the fourth century still proves to be substantially misleading. Two considerations are worth noting in this regard.

## This Claim Often Presupposes a Particularly Narrow Definition of the Term *Canon*

According to scholars like Hahneman, Sundberg, and Dungan, we must draw a sharp distinction between *canon* and *Scripture*. *Canon* is defined as a fixed, final, closed list of books, and therefore we cannot use the term until the boundaries of the canon are fully established.[16] Although *Scripture* would have existed prior

15. Dungan, *Constantine's Bible*, 133. The sentiment that Constantine produced the New Testament canon has been widely repeated in a variety of fictional literature, e.g., Dan Brown, *The Da Vinci Code* (New York: Doubleday, 2003), 231.

16. This particular definition of canon can be called the "exclusive" definition and is found in a number of modern works on canon: David H. Kelsey, *The Uses of Scripture in Recent Theology* (Philadelphia: Fortress Press, 1975), 104–5; James Barr, *The Scope and Authority of the Bible* (Philadelphia: Westminster, 1980), 120; Harry Y. Gamble, *The New Testament Canon: Its Making and Meaning* (Philadelphia: Fortress Press, 1985), 18–19; John Barton, "Canonical Approaches Ancient and Modern," in *The Biblical Canons*, ed. J.-M. Auwers and H. J. de Jonge (Leuven, Belg.: Leuven University Press, 2003), 202; Lee Martin McDonald, *The Formation of the Christian Biblical Canon* (Peabody, MA: Hendrickson, 1995), 13–21; Eugene Ulrich, "The Notion and Definition of Canon," in *The Canon Debate*, ed. Lee Martin McDonald and James A. Sanders (Peabody, MA: Hendrickson, 2002), 21–35; Craig D. Allert, *A High View of Scripture? The Authority of the Bible and the Formation of the New Testament Canon* (Grand Rapids: Baker Academic, 2007), 49–51; George Aichele, "Canon, Ideology, and the Emergence of an Imperial Church," in *Canon and Canonicity: The Formation*

to this period, these scholars argue that we must reserve the term *canon* until the end of the entire process. Thus, simply marshaling evidence of a book's scriptural status in the early church—as is so often done in canonical studies—is not enough for these scholars to consider it "canonical." The book must be part of a list from which nothing can be added or taken away. Given this narrow definition, one can understand how these scholars can say there is no canon until the fourth century. The problem, however, is that this historical "conclusion" is built in to the very definition itself.[17]

Of course, the average laymen in our congregations—and, to some extent, even our average pastors—are not aware of these underlying semantic debates. If these issues are left unaddressed, people are bound to get the impression that the development of the canon was much more problematic than it actually was. Indeed, that is the danger of such a strict Scripture-canon distinction—it gives the impression (whether intentional or not) that the state of the canon in the fourth century was radically different than in all preceding centuries; as if early Christians were utterly confused about what books to read until the church formally acted to declare what was in and what was out. Such a scenario inevitably presents the canon as something *created by* the church. Without the church, there could be no canon. For this reason, we must inform our congregations that the term *canon* can be applied prior to the fourth century, even if the boundaries were not yet fully solidified.[18]

---

*and Use of Scripture*, ed. Einar Thomassen (Copenhagen: Museum Tusculanum Press, 2010), 45–65; J. C. T. Barrera, "Origins of a Tripartite Old Testament Canon," in *The Canon Debate*, 128–45; and J. C. Poirier, "Scripture and Canon," in *The Sacred Text*, ed. Michael Bird and Michael Pahl (Piscataway, NJ: Gorgias Press, 2010), 83–98.

17. John Barton, *The Spirit and the Letter: Studies in the Biblical Canon* (London: SPCK, 1997), 1–34.

18. Critiques of the sharp Scripture-canon distinction can be found in Stephen B. Chapman, *The Law and the Prophets: A Study in Old Testament Canon Formation* (Tübingen: Mohr Siebeck, 2000), 71–110; idem, "How the Biblical Canon Began: Working Models and Open Questions," in *Homer, the Bible, and Beyond: Literary and Religious Canons in the Ancient World*, Jerusalem Studies in Religion and Culture 2, ed. Margalit Finkelberg and Guy G. Stroumsa (Leiden: Brill, 2003), 29–51; Iain Provan, "Canons to the Left of Him: Brevard Childs, His Critics, and the Future of

## This Claim Overlooks the Fact That There Was a "Core" Canon of New Testament Books by the Middle of the Second Century

Despite claims that the early stages of the canon were loose and wide open, the historical record suggests something very different. By the middle of the second century we see a solid core of New Testament books fully received as Scripture and operating with the highest level of authority for early Christians. This core is represented well by the late second-century Muratorian fragment, which recognized the four Gospels, Acts, the thirteen epistles of Paul, 1–2 John, Jude, and (to some extent) Revelation.[19] As Barton notes, "Astonishingly early, the great central core of the present New Testament was already being treated as the main authoritative source for Christians."[20] There was never really any doubt about these books nor was there any meaningful controversy over them. The vast majority of canonical debates among early Christians focused on the handful of "peripheral" books like 2 Peter, James, Hebrews, and 3 John.

Once we understand that there was a core New Testament by the middle of the second century, then the remaining challenges presented by the history of the canon are placed in their proper perspective. Even though Christians disagreed over some of these smaller books,

---

Old Testament Theology," *SJT* 50 (1997): 1–38; and Stephen G. Dempster, "Canons on the Right and Canons on the Left: Finding a Resolution in the Canon Debate," *JETS* 52 (2009): 51.

19. The date of the Muratorian fragment has been disputed by Albert C. Sundberg, "Canon Muratori: A Fourth-Century List," *HTR* 66 (1973): 1–41; and more recently by Hahneman, *The Muratorian Fragment*; and Lee Martin McDonald, *The Biblical Canon: Its Origin, Transmission, and Authority* (Peabody, MA: Hendrickson, 2007), 369–78. See responses from Charles E. Hill, "The Debate over the Muratorian Fragment and the Development of the Canon," *WTJ* 57 (1995): 437–52; Everett Ferguson, Review of *The Muratorian Fragment and the Development of the Canon*, by Geoffrey Mark Hahneman, *JTS* 44 (1993): 691–97; T. K. Heckel, *Vom Evangelium des Markus zum viergestaltigen Evangelium* (Tübingen: J. C. B. Mohr, 1999), 339–54; P. Henne, "La Datation du canon de Muratori," *RB* 100 (1993): 54–75; and J. Verheyden, "The Canon Muratori: A Matter of Dispute," in *The Biblical Canons*, 487–556.

20. Barton, *The Spirit and the Letter*, 18.

and even though some Christians occasionally used some apocryphal books, the existence of the core New Testament reminds us that the canonical foundation for early Christianity had *already* been laid. Regardless of the outcome of these minor debates, the core trajectory and the core teachings of Christianity were already established; the stories of Christ and the doctrines of Paul were already in place. Indeed, it was this very canonical foundation that was the basis for the future discussions about these other books—it was the standard by which all future decisions would be made. What is remarkable about the New Testament canon, then, is not that it took several centuries for the boundaries to be solidified (some disagreement is to be expected), but that the core New Testament was in place so early.

## THESIS #2: THE IDEA OF A WRITTEN NEW TESTAMENT WAS NOT INNATE TO EARLY CHRISTIANITY BUT A LATE SECOND-CENTURY IDEA IMPOSED UPON BOOKS WRITTEN FOR ANOTHER PURPOSE

Modern critics of canon are not content merely to challenge the date of the New Testament, but also are keen to challenge the basis for its very existence. Why do we even have a New Testament at all? Should there even be one? Even a brief survey of modern scholarly opinion reveals that the canon is often conceived of as something derived from church history.[21] It is an idea that the church has created and then retroactively imposed upon books originally written for another purpose. Its origins are not divine, but human. John Webster refers to such approaches as the "naturalization" of canon.[22]

21. D. Moody Smith, "When Did the Gospels Become Scripture?" *JBL* 119 (2000): 3–20, acknowledges that there is a widespread conviction among scholars that the New Testament books were not written to be Scripture: "The presumption of a historical distance, and consequent difference of purpose, between the composition of the NT writings and their incorporation into the canon of Scripture is representative of our discipline" (3).
22. John Webster, "'A Great and Meritorious Act of the Church'? The Dogmatic Location of the Canon," in *Die Einheit der Schrift und die Vielfalt des Kanons*, ed.

If the canon is nothing in and of itself, then it must be the result of contingent (and to some extent, arbitrary) human processes. Harnack is a prime example of this naturalization as he attributes the existence of the canon to the church's response to Marcion.[23] He declares, "No greater creative act can be mentioned in the whole history of the Church than the formation of the apostolic collection and the assigning to it of a position of equal rank with the Old Testament."[24] James Barr summarizes this approach: "The idea of a Christian faith governed by Christian written holy Scriptures was not an essential part of the foundation plan of Christianity."[25]

The problem with this particular thesis is that it is so myopically focused on canon as a product of church history that it misses the fact that canon ultimately has its roots in *redemptive history.* We shall argue that the theological and historical matrix of the first-century church was ideal for the production of a new corpus of canonical books. When the redemptive-historical era is examined more closely, it quickly becomes clear that the canon was a natural, early, and, to some extent, inevitable development. Two factors bear this out.

## The Pattern of Redemption

Throughout the Old Testament there is a pattern to God's redemptive activities: God acts to redeem his people, then he offers

---

John Barton and Michael Wolter (Berlin: Walter de Gruyter, 2003), 101.

23. Harnack's core thesis regarding Marcion was supported by Hans von Campenhausen, *The Formation of the Christian Bible* (London: Adam and Charles Black, 1972); German title: *Die Entstehung der christlichen Bibel* (Tübingen: J. C. B. Mohr, 1968). For other assessments of Marcion's influence on the canon, see R. Joseph Hoffmann, *Marcion: On the Restitution of Christianity: An Essay on the Development of Radical Paulinist Theology in the Second Century* (Chico, CA: Scholars Press, 1984); Barton, *The Spirit and the Letter*, 35–62; and Robert Grant, *The Formation of the New Testament* (New York: Harper & Row, 1965), 126.

24. Adolf von Harnack, *History of Dogma*, 3rd ed., trans. Neil Buchanan, 7 vols. (1894–1899; repr., New York: Dover, 1961), 2:62n1.

25. James Barr, *Holy Scripture: Canon, Authority and Criticism* (Philadelphia: Westminster, 1983), 12.

word-revelation to interpret, explain and apply that redemptive activity.[26] Vos observes this biblical pattern when he notes, "Revelation does not stand by itself, but is . . . inseparably attached to another activity of God, which we call *Redemption*."[27] This pattern is evident in the Exodus event itself. After God redeemed his people from Egypt he then offered them a new word-revelation that would establish his relationship with them (Exod. 20:2). If this is the case, then once Christians understood the work of Christ as the ultimate act of redemption—the great eschatological Exodus (Luke 9:31)—then they would have expected a new word-revelation from God to explain and interpret that event. Thus, it is the dawning of God's long-awaited redemptive triumph in the person of Jesus, and the new divine revelation related to that triumph, that is the impetus for the formation of the canon, not Marcion's heresies, Irenaeus's influence, or fourth-century ecclesiastical politics.

## The Structure of the Covenant

Of course, even if Christians anticipated new word-revelation to accompany the work of Christ, one might object that this does not imply that such revelation would be *written*. Perhaps it would be oral. However, Meredith Kline's work has challenged this notion. Kline has demonstrated that the Old Testament covenantal structure was patterned after treaty structures that were common in the Ancient Near East (particularly Hittite treaties).[28] Such covenants were always accompanied by written texts that

26. C. E. Hill, "The New Testament Canon: Deconstructio Ad Absurdum?" *JETS* 52 (2009): 105–6; Paul Helm, *The Divine Revelation: The Basic Issues* (London: Marshall, Morgan & Scott, 1982), 35.

27. Geerhardus Vos, *Biblical Theology* (Edinburgh: Banner of Truth, 1975), 5 (emphasis his).

28. Meredith G. Kline, *The Structure of Biblical Authority* (Eugene, OR: Wipf and Stock, 1997). See also G. E. Mendenhall, "Covenant Forms in Israelite Tradition," *BA* 17 (1954): 50–76; and Delbert R. Hillers, *Covenant: The History of a Biblical Idea* (Baltimore: Johns Hopkins University Press, 1969).

would affirm the terms of that covenant relationship. Given that the earliest Christians were immersed in the world of the Old Testament, we would naturally expect them to associate covenants with written texts. Indeed, Paul himself does this very thing when he describes the "Old Covenant" as something that people "read" (2 Cor. 3:14).[29] Covenant and canon go together. One implies the other. The ramifications of this are clear. If Christians believed that covenants had written texts, and if they believed that God had given them a new covenant—and they did believe this quite early[30]—then they would also have expected the new covenant to have written texts. Paul makes this connection between covenant and canon clear when he refers to himself and the other apostles as *diakonous kainēs diathēkēs* / διακόνους καινῆς διαθήκης ("ministers of a new covenant") within a *written* letter to the Corinthians (2 Cor. 3:6). In light of such a passage, it is difficult to avoid the implication that Paul understood the new covenant as having written texts just like the old (and that he played a role in writing them).

When the redemptive pattern of Scripture and the role of the covenant are understood, then we can see that conceptions of the canon as a merely a product of the early church fundamentally miss what canon really is. The canon was not an after-the-fact development, but something woven deep into the fabric of God's redemptive plan.

---

29. Peter Jensen, *The Revelation of God* (Downers Grove, IL: InterVarsity Press, 2002), 81.

30. E.g., Matt. 26:28; Mark 14:24; Luke 22:20; 1 Cor. 11:25; 2 Cor. 3:6, 14; Heb. 7:22; 8:6; *Barn.* 4.6–8; 13.1–6; 14.1–7; Justin Martyr, *Dial.* 11.1; 34.1; 43.1; 44.2; 51.3; 67.10; 122.5; Irenaeus, *Haer.* 1.10.3; 3.11.8; 4.9.1–3; 4.12.3. For the way patristic writers described New Testament writings as "covenant," see W. C. van Unnik, "ἡ καινή διαθήκη—A Problem in the Early History of the Canon," *StP* 4 (1961): 212–27; W. Kinzig, "καινή διαθήκη: The Title of the New Testament in the Second and Third Centuries," *JTS* 45 (1994): 519–44; Everett Ferguson, "The Covenant Idea in the Second Century," in *Texts and Testaments: Critical Essays on the Bible and the Early Church Fathers*, ed. W. Eugene March (San Antonio: Trinity University Press, 1980), 135–62.

## THESIS #3: THE AUTHORS OF THE NEW TESTAMENT DID NOT THINK THEY WERE WRITING "SCRIPTURE"

One of the most commonly heard refrains from some critical scholars is that the earliest writers of the New Testament had no idea they were writing "Scripture," nor were they aware of the authority of their own message. The writings we now call the New Testament were merely written as personal correspondence (in the case of epistles), or as reliable historical records (in the case of the Gospels and Acts). It was not until a later period—in the second or third centuries—that these writings began to attain any sort of status that would allow them to be called "Scripture." Lee McDonald declares, "[Paul] apparently was unaware of the divinely inspired status of his own advice. . . . He never wrote as if he himself were setting forth Scripture."[31] The import of such an approach is clear—it continues to present the New Testament canon as a late ecclesiastical phenomenon that is out of sync with the original intent of early Christians. Books are not written as Scripture, they only *become* Scripture when such a status is imposed on them.

As we evaluate this third challenge, we begin again by noting that it has an element of truth in it. No one would suggest that the New Testament authors would have foreseen the full and final scope of the twenty-seven-book New Testament canon and precisely understood their place in it. However, at the same time, we would be mistaken to think that the New Testament writers wrote without a sense of their own authority. Two considerations can help bring balance to our understanding of the New Testament authors' self-awareness.

### The Role of the Apostles

Missing from this critical approach to the New Testament canon is an appreciation for the role of the apostles as the mouthpieces of

---

31. McDonald, *The Biblical Canon*, 32.

Christ. The apostles were sent directly by Christ (Acts 10:41), with his full authority (John 20:21), to deliver his message to the nations (Matt. 28:19). And they were keenly aware that their message was authoritative not just in oral form, but also in written form (2 Thess. 2:15). Although numerous examples could be given, Paul made it quite explicit that he spoke not with the authority of men but with the direct authority of Christ (Gal. 1:1). At one point, Paul even declared, "If anyone thinks he is a prophet or spiritual, let him recognize that the things which I write (*graphō* / γράφω) to you are the Lord's commandment. But if anyone does not recognize *this*, he is not recognized" (1 Cor. 14:37–38). Paul not only equates his own authority with that of Jesus Christ, but specifically applies such authority to the *written* words of his letter, employing the term *graphō* / γράφω, which is often used elsewhere to refer to the written Scriptures. Moreover, Paul deems his spiritual authority to be so clear that he offers a "prophetic sentence of judgment" on all those who refuse to acknowledge it.[32] In light of a text such as this, it is difficult to imagine that McDonald is being fair with the New Testament data when he declares that Paul "was unaware of the divinely inspired status of his own advice."[33]

Such apostolic self-awareness would not be limited to books directly written by apostles. The key issue was not whether a book was physically penned by an apostle, but whether it bore authoritative apostolic *tradition*.[34] Thus, even a book like the Gospel of Luke was aware of its own apostolic authority as it attributed its content to "those who from the beginning were eyewitnesses and ministers of the word" (Luke 1:2).[35] In other words, Luke recognizes—and

32. Gordon D. Fee, *The First Epistle to the Corinthians*, New International Commentary on the New Testament (Grand Rapids: Eerdmans, 1987), 712.

33. McDonald, *The Biblical Canon*, 32.

34. Herman N. Ridderbos, *Redemptive History and the New Testament Scriptures*, trans. H. de Jongste, rev. Richard B. Gaffin Jr. (Phillipsburg, NJ: Presbyterian and Reformed, 1988), 32; Oscar Cullmann, "The Tradition," in *The Early Church* (London: SCM Press, 1956), 59–99.

35. Some central works on the prologue of Luke include Loveday Alexander, *The Preface to Luke's Gospel* (Cambridge: Cambridge University Press, 1993); Vernon K.

wants his audience to recognize—that his book bears the authoritative apostolic message.

## The New Testament Calls Itself *Scripture*

The idea that the New Testament books were not written as Scripture appears to be contradicted by some New Testament writers who seemed quite willing to assign scriptural status to other New Testament books. One of the earliest examples comes from the well-known passage in 2 Peter 3:16 in which Paul's letters are regarded as on a par with the *tas loipas graphas* / τὰς λοιπὰς γραφάς ("the other Scriptures") of the Old Testament. Most notably, this passage does not refer to just one letter of Paul, but to a *collection* of Paul's letters (how many is unclear) that had already begun to circulate throughout the churches—so much so that the author could refer to "all his [Paul's] letters" and expect that his audience would understand that to which he was referring.[36] Another noteworthy witness is 1 Timothy 5:18: "For the Scripture (*hē graphē* / ἡ γραφή) says, 'You shall not muzzle an ox when it treads out the grain,' and, 'The laborer

---

Robbins, "The Claims of the Prologues and Greco-Roman Rhetoric: The Prefaces to Luke and Acts in Light of Greco-Roman Rhetorical Strategies," in *Jesus and the Heritage of Israel*, ed. David P. Moessner (Harrisburg, PA: Trinity Press International, 1999), 63–83; Schuyler Brown, "The Role of the Prologues in Determining the Purpose of Luke-Acts," in *Perspectives on Luke-Acts*, ed. Charles H. Talbert (Edinburgh: T&T Clark, 1978), 99–111; and David E. Aune, "Luke 1:1–4: Historical or Scientific *Prooimion*?" in *Paul, Luke and the Graeco-Roman World: Essays in Honour of Alexander J. M. Wedderburn*, ed. Alf Christophersen et al. (Sheffield, UK: Sheffield Academic Press, 2002), 138–48.

36. Regarding Pauline letter collections see, David Trobisch, *Die Entstehung der Paulusbriefsammlung: Studien zu den Anfängen christlicher Publizistik (Novum testamentum et orbis antiquus)* (Göttingen: Vandenhoeck & Ruprecht, 1989); Stanley E. Porter, "When and How Was the Pauline Canon Compiled? An Assessment of Theories," in *The Pauline Canon*, ed. Stanley E. Porter (Leiden: Brill, 2004), 95–127; Harry Y. Gamble, "The Redaction of the Pauline Letters and the Formation of the Pauline Corpus," *JBL* 94 (1975): 403–18; K. L. Carroll, "The Expansion of the Pauline Corpus," *JBL* 72 (1953): 230–37; and C. Buck, "The Early Order of the Pauline Corpus," *JBL* 68 (1949): 351–57.

deserves his wages.' " The first citation is clearly derived from Deuteronomy 25:4, and the second is identical in wording to Luke 10:7, where it is found on the lips of Jesus. While some have wanted to attribute this citation to some apocryphal Gospel,[37] John Meier is correct when he declares, "The only interpretation that avoids contorted intellectual acrobatics or special pleading is the plain, obvious one. [First Timothy] is citing Luke's Gospel alongside Deuteronomy as normative Scripture for the ordering of the church's ministry."[38]

## THESIS #4: EARLY CHRISTIANITY WAS WILDLY DIVERSE—THEREFORE THE CANON IS SIMPLY THE BOOKS PREFERRED BY THE THEOLOGICAL WINNERS

Modern studies of the New Testament canon have been characterized by a relentless (if not near obsessive) focus on early Christian diversity.[39] Early Christianity was a theological mess, we are told, filled with competing Christian factions all trying to assert their dominance. There were no clear categories of "heresy" or "orthodoxy" and no clear majority view. There was no such thing as Christianity at this stage; instead there were *Christianities* (plural). Thus, we have no reason to think that the books that finally made it into the canon are necessarily representative of "original" Christianity. Instead, these books are simply the ones chosen by the "winners" of the power struggles in the early church. What about the competing Christian groups that lost? Who is to say their books are not just as valid?

37. J. N. D. Kelly, *A Commentary on the Pastoral Epistles* (Peabody, MA: Hendrickson, 1960), 126.

38. John P. Meier, "The Inspiration of Scripture: But What Counts as Scripture?" *Mid-Stream* 38 (1999): 77.

39. E.g., J. D. G. Dunn, *Unity and Diversity in the New Testament: An Inquiry into the Character of Early Christianity* (London: SCM Press, 1990); James M. Robinson and Helmut Koester, *Trajectories through Early Christianity* (Philadelphia: Fortress Press, 1971); Ehrman, *Lost Christianities*; McDonald, *Forgotten Scriptures*.

This entire line of thinking is not new. Rather, it comes from Walter Bauer's landmark 1934 book *Orthodoxy and Heresy in Earliest Christianity*.[40] Despite the fact that Bauer's thesis has been widely and definitively critiqued, it has gained new traction in the modern day. No doubt this resurgence of interest is due to the degree to which the thesis fits with postmodern worldviews that argue that there is no "right" or "wrong" version of any religious system.[41] For this reason, this particular argument against the canon may prove to be one of the most troubling for our congregations and therefore one of the most important for the church to address. Two considerations can help us respond to this challenge.

## The Diversity of Early Christianity Is Often Exaggerated

We need to acknowledge from the outset that certain parts of Bauer's thesis were correct. Indeed, early Christianity was diverse.

40. German title, *Rechtgläubigkeit und Ketzerei im ältesten Christentum* (Tübingen: J. C. B. Mohr, 1934). Bauer's thesis has been recently promoted on a number of fronts, including Helmut Koester, "Apocryphal and Canonical Gospels," *HTR* 73 (1980): 105–30; and Ehrman, *Lost Christianities*, 159–257. For a survey of its reception, see Daniel J. Harrington, "The Reception of Walter Bauer's *Orthodoxy and Heresy in Earliest Christianity* during the Last Decade," *HTR* 77 (1980): 289–98. Of course, Bauer been challenged over the years: see H. E. W. Turner, *The Pattern of Christian Truth: A Study in the Relations between Orthodoxy and Heresy in the Early Church* (London: A. R. Mowbray, 1954); Thomas Robinson, *The Bauer Thesis Examined: The Geography of Heresy in the Early Christian Church* (Lewiston, NY: Edwin Mellen, 1989); James McCue, "Orthodoxy and Heresy: Walter Bauer and the Valentinians," *VC* 33 (1979): 118–30; and I. Howard Marshall, "Orthodoxy and Heresy in Earlier Christianity," *Themelios* 2 (1976): 5–14. For a more recent critique of Bauer, see Andreas J. Köstenberger and Michael J. Kruger, *The Heresy of Orthodoxy: How Contemporary Culture's Fascination with Diversity Has Reshaped Our Understanding of Early Christianity* (Wheaton, IL: Crossway, 2010).

41. Helmut Koester, *Ancient Christian Gospels: Their History and Development* (London: SCM Press, 1990), draws heavily on Bauer's thesis and sounds quite postmodern when he argues that terms like *heresy* and *orthodoxy* should not be used because they reflect "discrimination" and "dogmatic prejudice" in favor of the canonical Gospels (xxx). Similarly, Ehrman, in *Lost Christianities*, shows his postmodern inclinations when he repeatedly chides orthodox Christianity (or "proto-orthodox," as he calls it) for being too "intolerant" of other religious systems (254–57). For a more thorough discussion (and critique) of postmodernity and its effects on Christianity, see D. A. Carson, *The Gagging of God: Christianity Confronts Pluralism* (Grand Rapids: Zondervan, 1996).

There were disagreements. There were battles between heresy and orthodoxy. Things were not always neat and tidy, and our congregations need to understand this. However, the amount of diversity within early Christianity tends to be significantly exaggerated by those in the Bauer camp. This is evident particularly in the discussion of apocryphal books. Critical scholars give the impression that apocryphal Gospels were dominant in early Christianity, making the canonical four just a small part of a larger group of writings that were widely used.[42] However, the number of manuscripts we possess of these Gospels does not substantiate this claim. Our extant manuscripts give us an indication of which books were popular and widely read by early Christian communities.[43] Compared to the high number of manuscripts of the canonical Gospels, Hurtado argues that the low number of apocryphal manuscripts "do not justify any notion that these writings were particularly favored" and that whatever circles used these writings "were likely a clear minority among Christians of the second and third centuries."[44]

### The Diversity Argument Includes a Key Hidden Assumption

In the midst of all these discussions about diversity, there is an assumption built into the argument that goes unstated and unproved: we can only believe we have the writings God intended if there are very few (if any) dissenters and virtually immediate and universal agreement on all twenty-seven canonical New Testament books. Put differently, if there are disagreements over books in the earliest stages of Christianity then we have no grounds for thinking the church got it right. But where does this assumption come from? And why should we think it is true? Does the presence of disagreement prove that no one view can be right? Not at all. Diversity

42. W. L. Petersen, "The Diatessaron and the Fourfold Gospel," in *The Earliest Gospels*, ed. Charles Horton (London: T&T Clark International, 2004), 51–52.

43. Larry W. Hurtado, *The Earliest Christian Artifacts: Manuscripts and Christian Origins* (Grand Rapids: Eerdmans, 2006), 15–41.

44. Ibid., 21–22.

itself is not an argument against canonicity. The mere *existence* of diversity and disagreement does not prove Bauer's case. Instead, the key issue is whether there is something distinctive about the canonical books that would allow them to be identified as such in the midst of that diversity. But the postmodern obsession with the Bauer thesis keeps this issue from ever being addressed. For one committed to a postmodern vision of history, a book's date, content, or historical merits are swept aside in favor of the belief that no book can be said to be more valid than any other.

## THESIS #5: THE AUTHORITY OF THE CANON IS DEPENDENT UPON THE AUTHORITY OF THE CHURCH

The idea that the authority of the canon is dependent on the authority of the church may sound like a Roman Catholic claim— and in many ways that is true. However, in recent years this claim has been widely made by many in critical scholarship, including some evangelicals. Craig Allert's recent work *A High View of Scripture?* is an example of this trend.[45] The stated goal of this volume is to "emphasize the centrality of the church in the formation of the New Testament."[46] To do so, Allert is keen to remind the reader that "the church existed before the Bible,"[47] and that the church was responsible for "forming our New Testament canon."[48] Thus, the overall thrust of Allert's book is that the canon is, in some sense, dependent upon the church. He concludes, "You cannot have a canon without the church."[49]

Now, we should state from the outset that much of Allert's intention here is commendable. No doubt, the ecclesiology of evangelicalism is shamefully low—the centrality of the church has been

45. Craig D. Allert, *A High View of Scripture? The Authority of the Bible and the Formation of the New Testament Canon* (Grand Rapids: Baker Academic, 2007).
46. Ibid., 67.
47. Ibid., 76.
48. Ibid., 77.
49. Ibid., 68.

replaced with a "me, God, and the Bible" type of individualism. In this sense, much of what Allert has to say is welcome. However, the concern here is not with the church having a role in the development of the canon but with the nature of that role. Is Allert's insistence that "you cannot have a canon without the church" the most helpful (and most biblical) way to articulate that role? It is not difficult to see how such a presentation of the church's role would present challenges to the average member of our congregations. How can we trust the canon if it is truly dependent on the church? With that as our starting point, we are forced in one of two directions. Either we conclude that the church is infallible (and become Roman Catholic), or we conclude that the canon is more of a human product than we might think. Allert himself seems to lean toward the latter option. Indeed, he expresses concern about how "verbal plenary theorists" have "come close to deifying this collection of texts" and how "the divinity of Scripture has virtually eclipsed the humanity."[50] How has this happened? According to Allert, it is because they have "little to no understanding of how [these texts] came to be collected into the Bible."[51] In other words, once we understand the complex history of the canon we will see the "human" side of the Bible more clearly.

The key to responding to such claims about the role of the church is to recover the Reformed understanding of the *self-authenticating* nature of Scripture.[52] Because the canonical books

50. Ibid., 11–12.

51. Ibid., 12.

52. Allert rejects this particular doctrine because, he argues, the early church fathers did not view inspiration as a quality that only canonical books possessed. He states, "The early church considered not only other documents inspired, but also many aspects of church life, including bishops, monks, interpreters of Scripture, martyrs, councils, and a wide array of prophetic gifts" (ibid., 59). However, there are two problems with Allert's argument: (a) He is too quick to assume that when the church fathers refer to other documents or people as *inspired*, they mean the term in the same manner as when it is applied to Scripture. Are we really to believe that the early fathers saw bishops as inspired in the same way as Scripture when they often tell us the exact opposite (e.g., 1 Clem. 42.1–2)? The language of inspiration can have different levels of meaning depending on the context. (b) Allert does not give

were constituted by the revelatory activity of the Holy Spirit, we would expect that there would be some evidence of that activity in the books themselves—the "imprint" of the Spirit, if you will.[53] Murray declares, "If . . . Scripture is divine in its origin, character, and authority, it must bear the marks or evidences of that divinity."[54] These "marks" (or *indicia*) can refer to a variety of things, but traditionally include Scripture's beauty, efficacy, and harmony.[55] Calvin himself understood that there were objective qualities evident within the canonical books that show they are from God: "It is easy to see that the Sacred Scriptures, which so far surpass all gifts and graces of human endeavor, breathe something divine."[56] Elsewhere he states, "Indeed, Scripture exhibits fully as clear evidence of its own truth as white and black things do of their color, or sweet and bitter things do of their taste."[57] Jesus himself affirmed this reality when he declared, "My sheep [i.e., those with the Spirit] hear my voice, and I know them, and they follow me" (John 10:27).

Once we understand the self-authenticating nature of Scripture, we begin to see the proper role of the church in the authentication of canon. The church's reception of these books is not evidence of its authority to choose the canon, as Allert and others maintain, but is evidence of the *opposite*, namely, the authority, power, and impact of the self-authenticating Scriptures to elicit a corporate

---

adequate attention to the fact that some church fathers were simply mistaken about some books being inspired (e.g., the Shepherd of Hermas). The fact that there were occasional instances of disagreements among church fathers does not invalidate the self-authenticating nature of Scripture because we have no reason to think that the self-authenticating nature of Scripture would produce *absolute* agreement amongst believers with no exceptions. There could be pockets of disagreement in the midst of a larger church-wide consensus.

53. Richard A. Muller, *PPRD*, 2:270–302; J. I. Packer, *Fundamentalism and the Word of God* (Grand Rapids: Eerdmans, 1992), 115–25.

54. John Murray, "The Attestation of Scripture," in *The Infallible Word: A Symposium by the Members of the Faculty of Westminster Theological Seminary*, ed. N. B. Stonehouse and Paul Woolley (Philadelphia: Presbyterian and Reformed, 1946), 46.

55. WCF 1.5.

56. John Calvin, *Institutes*, 1.8.1.

57. Ibid., 1.7.2.

response from the church. The church's full affirmation of these books does not show that it created or constituted the canon, but *is the natural and inevitable outworking of the self-authenticating nature of Scripture.* Jesus' statement that "My sheep hear my voice . . . and they follow me" (John 10:27) is not evidence for the authority of the sheep's decision to follow, but evidence for the authority and efficacy of the Shepherd's voice to call.[58] After all, the act of hearing is, by definition, derivative not constitutive.[59] Thus, when the canon is understood as self-authenticating, it is clear that the church did not choose the canon, but the canon, in a sense, chose itself.[60] As Childs has noted, the content of these writings "exerted an authoritative *coercion* on those receiving their word."[61] Barth agrees: "The Bible constitutes itself the Canon. It is the Canon because it *imposed itself* upon the Church."[62] In this way, then, the role of the church is like a thermometer, not a thermostat. Both instruments provide information about the temperature in the room—but one determines it and one reflects it.

The self-authenticating nature of the canon reminds us that the church is always the *creatura verbi* ("creation of the Word").[63] Such an approach is precisely the opposite of the one advocated by Allert. He has argued that "you cannot have a canon without the

58. John Calvin, *Tracts and Treatises*, trans. Henry Beveridge (Grand Rapids: Eerdmans, 1958), 267.

59. John Webster, *Holy Scripture: A Dogmatic Sketch* (Cambridge: Cambridge University Press, 2003), 45; see also C. Schwöbel, "The Creature of the Word: Recovering the Ecclesiology of the Reformers," in *On Being the Church: Essays on the Christian Community*, ed. Colin E. Gunton and Daniel W. Hardy (Edinburgh: T&T Clark, 1989), 110–55.

60. Dunn, *Unity and Diversity in the New Testament*, xxxi.

61. Brevard S. Childs, "The One Gospel in Four Witnesses," in *The Rule of Faith: Scripture, Canon, and Creed in a Critical Age*, ed. Ephraim Radner and George Sumner (Harrisburg, PA: Morehouse, 1998), 53 (emphasis added).

62. Karl Barth, *Church Dogmatics*, 2nd ed., 14 vols., trans. G. W. Bromiley and T. F. Torrance (Edinburgh: T&T Clark, 1975), 1.1.107 (emphasis added).

63. Michael S. Horton, *People and Place: A Covenant Ecclesiology* (Louisville: Westminster John Knox, 2008), 37–71; and John Webster, "The Self-Organizing Power of the Gospel of Christ: Episcopacy and Community Formation," in *Word and Church: Essays in Church Dogmatics* (Edinburgh: T&T Clark, 2001), 191–210.

church." On the contrary, we would argue that "you cannot have a church without the canon."

## Conclusion

We began our discussion with an observation by Kurt Aland that the issue of canon "is one which confronts not only the New Testament scholar, but every Christian theologian."[64] This includes the average church member in the pew. If we are to help that person withstand the modern critical challenges to canon, we need to know what those challenges are. In the above survey we have looked at five main tenets of modern canonical studies:

1. There was no "canon" until the fourth century.
2. The idea of a written New Testament was not innate to early Christianity but a late second-century idea imposed upon books written for another purpose.
3. The New Testament writers did not think they were writing Scripture.
4. Early Christianity was wildly diverse—therefore the canon is simply the books of the theological winners.
5. The authority of the canon is dependent on the authority of the church.

Given the significance of these challenges to the integrity of the canon, we should make it a priority to educate our congregations about matters such as this. Although our average church member has a high view of the Bible, there is often very little understanding of the origins of the Bible. By probing into the Bible's origins, every Christian will be confronted with the critical themes of redemptive history, revelation, the work of the Spirit, and God's sovereignty over history. This will renew our confidence that Christ was correct when he promised, "My sheep hear my voice and I know them, and they follow me" (John 10:27).

64. Aland, *The Problem of the New Testament Canon*, 31.

# 4

# Inerrancy's Complexities: Grounds for Grace in the Debate

ROBERT W. YARBROUGH

## THE HERITAGE OF THE DOCTRINE OF BIBLICAL INERRANCY: THE CHICAGO STATEMENT

Why "complexities" in this essay's title? In this section and in the next, we will see that in some ways there is nothing very complex about this doctrine. A terse definition of it comes from church historian John Woodbridge, who notes that among other things inerrancy means "the Bible is infallible for faith and practice as well as for matters of history and science."[1] A fuller definition is found in the five points of "A Short Statement," which appears at the beginning of the 1978 Chicago

---

1. John Woodbridge, "Evangelical Self-Identity and the Doctrine of Biblical Inerrancy," in *Understanding the Times: New Testament Studies in the 21st Century: Essays in Honor of D. A. Carson on the Occasion of His 65th Birthday*, ed. Andreas Köstenberger and Robert W. Yarbrough (Wheaton, IL: Crossway, 2011), 107.

Statement on Biblical Inerrancy.[2] We need to revisit this fuller sense as a reminder that the doctrine in recent formulation by its proponents is not merely about factual accuracy, though that is not unimportant. Inerrancy as a description of God's Word, the Bible, relates first of all to God who gave that Word,[3] and then in a derivative sense to the written Word he has given. Inerrancy is a *theological* doctrine, having to do with the living God and not only the Book associated with his name.

Article 1 of "A Short Statement" highlights this as it states:

> 1. God, who is Himself Truth and speaks truth only, has inspired Holy Scripture in order thereby to reveal Himself to lost mankind through Jesus Christ as Creator and Lord, Redeemer and Judge. Holy Scripture is God's witness to Himself.

We see that not only is inerrancy, as defined in perhaps the twentieth century's most publicized statement on the subject,[4] God-centered, as already noted; it is also soteriologically oriented. It is interwoven with the redemptive aim of human salvation. Further, it is christocentric, affirming Christ's revelatory centrality for lost humanity. This is all worth noting, because the Chicago Statement has been charged with being a rationalistic document, an icon of a sterile, biblicistic fundamentalism. Possibly it has been used this way. But is that really how the document reads? Let us take a look at the other articles in the statement's preface.

2. Chicago Statement on Biblical Inerrancy, accessed May 17, 2011, http://www.reformed.org/documents/index.html?mainframe=http://www.reformed.org/documents/icbi.html. This document is available at many online locations. For a comparable definition more recently, see *Evangelical Convictions: A Theological Exposition of the Statement of Faith of the Evangelical Free Church of America* (Minneapolis: Free Church Publications, 2011), 3.

3. Cf. Paul Helm and Carl Trueman, eds., *The Trustworthiness of God: Perspectives on the Nature of Scripture* (Grand Rapids: Eerdmans, 2002).

4. For an important evaluation of the Chicago Statement, see Jason Sexton, "How Far beyond Chicago? Assessing Recent Attempts to Reframe the Inerrancy Debate," *Themelios* 34, 1 (2009): 26–49.

2. Holy Scripture, being God's own Word, written by men prepared and superintended by His Spirit, is of infallible divine authority in all matters upon which it touches: it is to be believed, as God's instruction, in all that it affirms; obeyed, as God's command, in all that it requires; embraced, as God's pledge, in all that it promises.

This article reminds us that inerrancy is about *faith*: the Bible is to be believed. Its truth value is neglected or abused when it does not lead to personal trust in the God who gave it. Inerrancy is also about *ethics*: the Bible is to be obeyed. Its truth value is neglected or abused when confessed Bible believers disregard its directives. Inerrancy is also about *love of God*. Language like "embraced" and "God's pledge" and "promises" brings us into a relational context. This is relation with a God who is love (1 John 4:8) and who calls love for him the greatest commandment (Deut. 6:5; Matt. 22:36, 38; 1 Cor. 13:13). An inerrant Bible's truth value is neglected or abused when what Scripture says is not relationally "embraced." For it is, in the Chicago Statement's view, a loving "God's pledge" to us, an extended and complex presentation of his "promises" to his beloved people and to all the world.

3. The Holy Spirit, Scripture's divine Author, both authenticates it to us by His inward witness and opens our minds to understand its meaning.

This article, with its stress on the Holy Spirit, confirms the Trinitarian underpinning of the Chicago Statement, Father and Son having been central in the two previous articles. It also affirms the spiritual quality of the Bible's existence, God's Spirit being its ultimate author. And it centers not human rationality but divine operation as the means by which Scripture confirms its truth to readers and discloses its meaning. Just as Lydia's heart was opened at Philippi (Acts 16:14), our hearts and minds are opened by the work of God's Spirit to receive what Scripture is and what it tells us. Inerrancy is not a doctrine designed to subordinate Scripture to religious hierarchies that wield its authority to their advantage. Inerrancy rather affirms human subordination to the Spirit who gives Scripture, confirms its veracity to us, enables us to comprehend its claims, and unites us with God's people in all ages and indeed with God himself.

> 4. Being wholly and verbally God-given, Scripture is without error or fault in all its teaching, no less in what it states about God's acts in creation, about the events of world history, and about its own literary origins under God, than in its witness to God's saving grace in individual lives.

This article brings us to the crux of what inerrancy is most commonly taken to be about when the doctrine is discussed, especially by its critics: the Bible is errorless and faultless with respect to all that it affirms and teaches. (This assumes proper interpretation of any given passage.) Many among even church leaders do not believe this but find errors in the Bible. So it is understandable that they seize on this point to attack the doctrine of inerrancy. This is not the place to reply to those attacks. But we should reiterate that this article is not the only article and not even the first one but the fourth of five. Characterizations of the inerrancy doctrine that stress this article to the minimizing of others are misguided. This is true for both detractors from and defenders of the doctrine.

> 5. The authority of Scripture is inescapably impaired if this total divine inerrancy is in any way limited or disregarded, or made relative to a view of truth contrary to the Bible's own; and such lapses bring serious loss to both the individual and the Church.

This article affirms inerrancy's significance in three ways. First, to limit or disregard inerrancy is to impair Scripture's authority. Second, when a view of truth foreign to the Bible is used to interpret the Bible, biblical authority suffers. Third, there are negative personal and ecclesial consequences when the "high" view of Scripture associated with inerrancy is displaced by a "low" view that takes a dimmer view of Scripture's comprehensive veracity.

Elsewhere in the preface to the Chicago Statement, its authors conceded, "We gladly acknowledge that many who deny the inerrancy of Scripture do not display the consequences of this denial in the rest of their belief and behavior." Inerrancy is not an essential doctrine in the same sense that Christ's resurrection is, or his full divinity and humanity. Yet it is barely less than essential. Inerrancy is arguably the teaching of Scripture about itself. Inerrancy articulates what prophets, apostles, and the Lord Jesus himself held to be true about God's written Word. As we will show in the next section, inerrancy has been the historic teaching of most of the Western church through almost its whole history. There is reason to suppose that there is little of positive value to be gained by giving up the doctrine now.

So far we have looked at a few aspects of the heritage of the doctrine of biblical inerrancy and briefly reviewed the prefatory five articles of the Chicago Statement as a means of reminding ourselves that the doctrine in this well-known formulation of the previous generation is not as austere and bloodless as may occasionally be implied. While the doctrine and those who hold it are on occasion maligned, this is often because just one slice of inerrancy's concern (Article 4) gets inordinate attention. Such misplaced attention disregards important nuances of the Chicago Statement found in the other articles and elsewhere and makes it hard to understand why this doctrine has been assumed, defended, and echoed by so many church leaders from so many quarters over the centuries.

This leads to our next section. It is commonly affirmed that biblical inerrancy is a novel teaching, developed by fundamentalists or, at least, fundamentalist impulses surging forth from the intellectual backwaters of North America in the last few generations. But is this assumption true?

ROBERT W. YARBROUGH

## THE HISTORY OF THE DOCTRINE OF BIBLICAL
## INERRANCY

John Woodbridge, church history professor at Trinity Evangelical Divinity School, has played a key role in defending the doctrine of inerrancy for some thirty years.[5] He recently performed the great service of bringing his argument up to date in important respects. He notes that a new view of biblical inerrancy has established itself today in many circles. In this view, inerrancy is "a doctrinal innovation."[6] It arose in American fundamentalism. Whereas in the 1970s there was consensus among most evangelicals that inerrancy was a nonnegotiable article of Christian confession,[7] by the 1980s, through the influence of Ernest Sandeen[8] and others, the view became popular that A. A. Hodge and B. B. Warfield created the doctrine in an article they penned in 1881.[9] Sandeen claimed that the doctrine "did not exist in either Europe or America prior to its formulation in the last half of the nineteenth century."[10] I think it is fair to say that if this were true, many of us would be nervous now about documents like the Chicago Statement and about movements like the Presbyterian Church in America (PCA), which uphold a high view of Scripture and do not shy away from using words like *inerrant* and *infallible* to characterize the Bible.

5. See especially his *Biblical Authority: A Critique of the Rogers/McKim Proposal* (Grand Rapids: Zondervan, 1982). See also the two volumes Woodbridge edited with D. A. Carson: *Scripture and Truth* (Grand Rapids: Baker, 1992); *Hermeneutics, Authority, and Canon* (Eugene, OR: Wipf and Stock, 2005).
6. Woodbridge, "Evangelical Self-Identity and the Doctrine of Biblical Inerrancy," 107.
7. Ibid., 108.
8. See particularly Ernest R. Sandeen, *The Origins of Fundamentalism: Toward a Historical Interpretation* (Philadelphia: Fortress Press, 1968); idem, *The Roots of Fundamentalism: British and American Millenarianism, 1800–1930* (Chicago: University of Chicago Press, 1970).
9. Woodbridge, "Evangelical Self-Identity and the Doctrine of Biblical Inerrancy," 108–9.
10. Ibid., 109.

But Woodbridge revisits the historical sources to test Sandeen's hypothesis. Woodbridge's thesis is that biblical inerrancy has been a "central teaching of the Western Christian churches, including evangelical Protestant churches," going back at least to Augustine.[11] He cites Hans Küng's remark that "Augustine's influence in regard to inspiration and inerrancy prevailed throughout the Middle Ages and right into the modern age."[12] Küng, at least, believes that inerrancy was not invented by Old Princeton. Woodbridge cites a lengthy passage from Augustine illustrating his affirmation of a Bible free from error;[13] I will summarize the quote Woodbridge uses with another Augustine quote:

> The authority of the divine Scriptures becomes unsettled (so that every one may believe what he wishes, and reject what he does not wish) if this be once admitted, that the men by whom these things have been delivered unto us, could in their writings state some things which were not true.[14]

In another passage Augustine writes of "the canonical books of Scripture" that

> Of these alone do I most firmly believe that the authors were completely free from error. And if in these writings I am perplexed by anything which appears to me opposed to truth, I do not hesitate to suppose that either the manuscript is faulty, or the translator has not caught the meaning of what was said, or I myself have failed to understand it.[15]

Woodbridge shows that this general view of Scripture can be documented in Luther's contemporary Johannes Eck (1496–1543).[16]

11. Ibid., 107.

12. Ibid., 110–11, citing Hans Küng, *Infallible? An Enquiry* (London: Collins, 1972), 174.

13. Ibid., 111; Woodbridge cites Augustine, *Letters of St. Augustine*, 28.3.

14. Augustine, *Letters of St. Augustine*, 28.5.

15. Ibid., 82.3.

16. Woodbridge, "Evangelical Self-Identity and the Doctrine of Biblical Inerrancy," 113–15.

In the century following Eck the man who has been called "the father of higher criticism," Richard Simon (1638–1712), asserted in 1678 that "all Jews and Christians . . . [believe] in the divine authority and infallibility of Scripture because it came from God."[17] At about this same time the German pietist Albrecht Bengel was among Protestant scholars speaking of the error-free nature of the original manuscripts (*autographa*);[18] Bengel's zeal to arrive at pristine readings of the original writings so far as these can be determined is part of what drove him to become one of the earliest great New Testament textual critics.[19]

Pope Leo XIII in the nineteenth century was saying much the same thing as Hodge and Warfield were, but probably not due to Protestant, American, or fundamentalist considerations.[20] Pope Pius XII affirmed the historic Catholic and Augustinian view in 1943.[21] The same view was present in the first draft of the Constitution on Divine Revelation in Vatican II documents in the early 1960s.[22] It is at this point that some Roman Catholic scholars start to veer away from their own church's historic teaching, so that the eventually published documents of Vatican II sound rather different notes. But many Catholic leaders thought then and think now that the shift was a mistake.[23]

Having established the virtual universality of an inerrantist view of Scripture in the Catholic church (with general Protestant concurrence) until recently, Woodbridge then asks more pointedly whether this was also the view of the Protestant Reformers and their descendents. He shows that from Luther and Thomas Cran-

17. Ibid., 116.

18. Ibid., 116–17, cf. 130.

19. Cf. Bruce Metzger and Bart Ehrman, *The Text of the New Testament*, 4th ed. (New York: Oxford University Press, 2005), 112. See also Alan Thompson, "Pietist Critique of Inerrancy? J. A. Bengel's *Gnomon* as a Test Case," *JETS* 47 (2004): 79–80.

20. Woodbridge, "Evangelical Self-Identity and the Doctrine of Biblical Inerrancy," 117–20.

21. Ibid., 120.

22. Ibid., 121.

23. Cf. ibid., 122n53.

mer forward, the Catholic view of Scripture (though not of church tradition) was seen to be the true view, taught in Scripture itself and upheld through the centuries.[24] This view continues through Calvin and in the Reformation's wake among the Protestant orthodox.[25] William Whitaker affirms inerrancy in 1588.[26] Samuel Taylor Coleridge laments that this is the view of most English Protestants as of the 1830s.[27] Later in the nineteenth century, Louis Auguste Sabatier (1839–1901) documents that many French and Swiss Protestants upheld inerrancy into the 1840s.[28] Frédérick Louis Godet (1812–1900) exemplifies a high view of Scripture among Reformed Francophones extending to the twentieth century.[29] Thomas Huxley (1825–95), Darwin's defender, "acknowledged that the vast majority of the English people had believed in biblical infallibility in earlier decades."[30] It is worth noting that Sabatier and Huxley also mention the rise of an attempt to affirm some kind of limited inerrancy view, in which Scripture would be true in some ways about some things but at the same time empirically false based on canons of current thought and convictions.[31] Both men note the inherent contradiction of the notion of a Bible that is totally true to a certain extent. They pronounce the move ill-conceived, not because they believed in the Bible—they didn't—but because it marked a break with historic understanding as well as logic.

In sum, A. A. Hodge and B. B. Warfield did not invent the doctrine of inerrancy nor the conviction that inerrancy refers in the first instance to the autographs. From Augustine through the

24. Ibid., 122–24.
25. Ibid., 124–26.
26. Ibid., 126–27.
27. Ibid., 131.
28. Ibid., 131–32.
29. Cf. Robert W. Yarbrough, "Godet, Frédéric Louis," in *Dictionary of Major Biblical Interpreters*, ed. Donald K. McKim (Downers Grove, IL: IVP Academic, 2007), 465–69.
30. Woodbridge, "Evangelical Self-Identity and the Doctrine of Biblical Inerrancy," 132.
31. Ibid., 132–33.

Reformers to Bengel and on to the current hour, it can be said, as Woodbridge observes, that over the past two millennia

> countless Roman Catholics and evangelical Protestants believed that the Bible was infallible not only for matters of faith and practice but also for history and science. Augustine's teaching in this regards was tantamount to an essential church doctrine for many Roman Catholics and Protestants. Some claimed this belief flowed directly from the premise that God, the author of truth, is also the ultimate author of Holy Scripture. Thus Scripture is without error. Many believed the doctrine served as a strong guardrail against the possibility of slipping or plunging into heterodoxy or worse. Many assumed it was a non-negotiable belief of their evangelical theological identity.[32]

## OUR APPROPRIATION OF THE DOCTRINE OF BIBLICAL INERRANCY

It is now time to take up the "complexities" of inerrancy mentioned in this essay's title and our grounds for grace in inerrancy discussions. Confessionally (meaning the Reformed and WCF heritage)[33] and in-house (meaning in the PCA), the inerrancy position is secure. As we have seen, this view is credibly articulated in documents like the Chicago Statement and consistently confessed by church leaders through the centuries. If we had space, we could discuss how inerrancy flows inexorably from the testimony of God-breathed Scripture itself, including Christ's testimony to Scripture, an aspect of his authority widely minimized today, with some Christians feeling much braver about departing from the whole truth of all God's written Word than the Son of God himself did. Strong

---

32. Ibid., 135.

33. For defense of the proposition that the WCF affirms an infallible/inerrant Bible (the terms were interchangeable at that time in the English language), see, e.g., Rowland S. Ward, "Recent Criticisms of the Westminster Confession of Faith," accessed May 31, 2011, at http://www.spindleworks.com/library/wcf/ward.htm.

justifying hints of an inerrantist view of the Bible are as common in Scripture as this statement by Solomon that I ran across in recent daily Bible readings: "Blessed be the LORD who has given rest to his people Israel, according to all that he promised. Not one word has failed of all his good promise, which he spoke by Moses his servant" (1 Kings 8:56). A verse from Proverbs for that same day runs, "Every word of God proves true; he is a shield to those who take refuge in him" (Prov. 30:5). I realize that many make a hard separation between "word of God" and written Scripture, but that is an Enlightenment deviation from church and biblical teaching that I have never found compelling.

And yet complexities do attach to inerrancy convictions. For ours is a missionary faith, extending outward across communities and continents, and for us in the increasingly pagan United States boomeranging back to us from countries of the global South that now send missionaries here. It also stretches forth into coming generations. As gospel tidings flow throughout the world and impact those who will shape the decades ahead, inerrancy faces stiff challenges, not only from outside church circles but also from within. How do we balance a commitment to inerrancy with a suitably humble and gracious articulation of the inerrancy position? Following is a list of just seven challenges to the doctrine that we do well to keep in mind as we move into the future. Many more, of course, could be listed.

## "The Innovationist Edge"[34]

About twenty years ago Richard John Neuhaus, appealing to Gilbert Meilaender, noted that "the things that are most important to living a good life elude our sure analytical grasp." The goodness of marriage or the heinousness of child molestation seem self-evident. Then along comes the fashionable iconoclast, who, in Neuhaus's words,

34. Cf. Richard John Neuhaus, "The Innovationist Edge," *First Things* (November 1992), accessed May 31, 2011, at http://www.firstthings.com/article/2008/03/the-innovationist-edge-43. Quotes in this paragraph refer to this source.

81

not only has the frisson of being revolutionary, but . . . can indulge the conceit of being intellectually superior since he has examined what others take for granted. "Give me three good arguments against incest," he challenges. And his poor interlocutor has to admit he really hasn't given the matter that much thought. The fact that decent people have always thought incest a very bad thing does not count as a good argument.

Historically speaking, a view of Scripture that challenges its entire and detailed truthfulness is an innovation. Most notably since the Enlightenment, it became increasingly common from within ecclesial circles (skeptics have always discounted the Scriptures) to doubt or radically reinterpret biblical and church teaching on this subject. Objections to inerrancy sprout, grow to tree-size stature, and then are felled, only to be replaced in a subsequent generation by sprouts from the stump. We can look for this cycle of innovationism to continue. There will always be ways for new authorities who advocate less confidence in the whole counsel of canonical Scripture to present themselves as angels of light. In the nature of the case, inerrantist responses will always be subject to the charge of being defensive and reactionary. Cultivating this appearance is usually part of the strategy and adds to the innovationist appeal among the like-minded.

## Well-Meaning but Ill-Advised Inerrantist Zealotry

It is easy for those who affirm inerrancy to overreact to challenges to the Bible's authority. This is one reason why the Chicago Statements on inerrancy, and its sequel on hermeneutics, go to some lengths to qualify their inerrancy outlook. It is easy to overplay one's hand and come off looking foolish. Perhaps one does not really know the issues. Perhaps the innovator is simply more clever at some point of challenge. Perhaps there is no known, agreed-on solution to a long-standing or freshly-minted conundrum.[35] When proponents of

35. E.g., Luke is commonly faulted for misdating the Quirinius census, with Josephus telling the story correctly. But the case is not yet closed; see John H. Rhoads,

inerrancy defend their view with too much haste and bluster and not enough substance, it gives credence to proposals that Scripture errs after all. It is very easy for the smooth stone of inerrancy conviction to miss the forehead of the Goliath of Bible skepticism.

One form that inerrantist zealotry can take is confusion of the Bible's confessed inerrancy with the inerrancy of defenders of the doctrine. In the Chicago Statement's opening section we read these wise words: "We claim no personal infallibility for the witness we bear, and for any help which enables us to strengthen this testimony to God's Word we shall be grateful."[36] We see here an attempt, at least, to give full credence to Scripture while claiming no monopoly on wisdom and truth based on mere human resources. Even with this disclaimer in place, it has been easy for inerrancy's detractors to impute bad faith and petty self-righteousness to inerrancy's upholders. Sometimes the detractors have been justified.

**Failure to Love Enemies and Pray for Persecutors**

It is natural for the flesh to bridle when what we think is right is challenged. It is not so easy to *care about* the individuals and enclaves who are perceived or real opponents of Christian teaching. And yet as with all significant articles of Christian faith, a work of divine grace is needed for eyes to be opened and for the Bible's truth in its fullest dimensions to be acknowledged. There are things that no amount of evidence can "prove" unless attended by the suasion of divine influence. The anger of man, however correct biblically and empirically an angry person may be, does not achieve the righteousness of God. Those involved in disputes regarding biblical authority cannot hope to prevail without God working on their behalf. Grieve the Spirit and you can hardly count on his robust support. Lovelessness and prayerlessness are among cardinal errors that anyone toiling

"Josephus Misdated the Census of Quirinius," *JETS* 54, 1 (March 2011): 65–87. Presumed biblical errors may simply await discovery of new evidence or more careful observation of available data.

36. See footnote 2 above.

in favor of any biblical truths (including the gospel message itself) can commit. It is particularly easy to fall into unholy derision and barren polemics in inerrancy discussions.

## Other Priorities in Other Parts of the World

We are living in the wake of the largest numeric expansion of world Christian population ever witnessed. On the one hand, the new gospel-believing communities tend toward a higher rather than a lower view of Scripture. This is shown, for example, by Philip Jenkins in *The New Faces of Christianity: Believing the Bible in the Global South*.[37] And yet this is not because of the advance of an explicitly inerrantist agenda. The fact is that no one can explain for sure the explosion of Christianity in South America, Africa, and Asia over the last century. We *can* say, as Mark Noll has argued, that this explosion has much in common with the North American evangelical expression of the Christian faith.[38] It was not due primarily to money, military might, or other blandishments of US "empire." It seems rather the case that values and beliefs that evangelicals find in Scripture have played a key role. From another direction, Lamin Sanneh has argued in *Whose Religion Is Christianity? The Gospel Beyond the West*[39] that throughout the world there has been local rediscovery of biblical claims that are not Western in origin or parasitic on the West in expression. I do not recall "inerrancy" being mentioned in Sanneh's study, or in Noll's for that matter.[40]

While much could be said about this complex state of affairs, the point I wish to underscore is that inerrancy debates per se have not been at the forefront of this global expansion. Those for whom

37. Philip Jenkins, *The New Faces of Christianity: Believing the Bible in the Global South* (New York: Oxford University Press, 2006).

38. See Mark Noll, *The New Shape of World Christianity: How American Experience Reflects Global Faith* (Downers Grove, IL: IVP Academic, 2009).

39. Lamin Sanneh, *Whose Religion Is Christianity? The Gospel beyond the West* (Grand Rapids: Eerdmans, 2003).

40. Mention of a high view of Scripture does occur in Noll, *The New Shape of World Christianity*, 13, 152.

inerrancy is important should use caution about viewing what may be high priority in our locales as integral to Christian nurture and growth in other settings. Personally, in my more than fifteen years of involvement in pastoral training in Arab Muslim contexts in Africa, "inerrancy" has never come up. The Bible's truth and Jesus Christ's authority in the face of rival Islamic and native African claims are simply assumed by the African churches and believers I have served. We teach about Christ and him crucified and risen based broadly on the Bible's testimony. Jesus is the issue and faith in him is the need, with a high doctrine of Scripture assumed but not explicitly delineated in formal terms like we see in the Chicago Statement or even in the WCF. Is this a pointer to a trap that lurks if the *inerrancy* of Scripture were to overshadow *the saving message* of Scripture? In a quarter century of teaching seminary and graduate students in the United States, I think I *have* seen students, and perhaps a few pastors and professors, who seemed marked more by zeal for inerrancy than by the full range of graces imparted by the Holy Spirit. The growth of world Christianity may help us keep inerrancy debates in perspective.

## Leaders in the Church and Academy Who Do Not Know Jesus

A vignette in the January 25, 2011, issue of *Christian Century* reminds us that many who teach the Bible even to ministry students lack personal knowledge of Jesus.[41] This is self-evident from the writings of some today who openly disavow Christian teaching and teach the Bible from perspectives hostile to Christian understanding of it. But this little *Christian Century* piece tells the brave story of a New Testament professor at a Mennonite seminary who for over twenty years taught her subject with some disdain for the notion of a personal relationship with the one who died to forgive sins. But through novel teaching circumstances, this professor writes, "I found Jesus—and some of the old evangelical language I had

41. See pages 10–11 of this issue. I omit the name out of courtesy and respect for the person who published this courageous autobiographical account.

foresworn seemed newly relevant to the somewhat jaded and shop-worn New Testament professor that I had become."

This incident reminds us of our Western cultural setting in which academic and often ecclesial hegemony belongs to persons and forces who reject the biblical and Reformation gospel, never mind the doctrine of biblical inerrancy. A few years back a round-table discussion published in *Biblical Archaeology Review* docu-mented, in the words of scholars themselves, how academic study of the Bible contributed to the destruction of Christian faith in Bart Ehrman and in John Devers, two widely published Bible scholars.[42] A third scholar who is a Baptist minister denies Jesus' bodily resur-rection in the same discussion. We might draw many corollaries from this, but one is surely that here in the United States no less than on the world scene, we need to use discernment in the ways we articulate our high view of Scripture. We may think we are simply honoring Christ. But people, including highly intelligent and trained people, who do not know Christ can hardly avoid seeing something quite different than what we intend. This does not mean that we should never articulate our convictions about Scripture to those who appear to be hostile or oblivious to Scripture's witness to Jesus. But as Paul lamented the recalcitrance of his fellow Jews, we do well to cultivate empathy with respect to settings where Scripture is wit-tingly or unwittingly opposed. There but by grace go we. And as evangelicalism moves deeper into decades of its own institutional hegemony in various spheres, we are not free from the bane of nominal Christians in our own circles, including our leadership.

## Hypocrisy among Inerrantists

It is a truism that we are often our own worst enemies. David Hempton's book *Evangelical Disenchantment: Nine Portraits of Faith*

---

42. See Hershel Shanks, "Losing Faith: Who Did and Who Didn't. How Scholar-ship Affects Scholars," *BAR* 33, 2 (March–April 2007): 50–57.

*and Doubt*[43] recounts the fall from evangelical belief in bygone generations on the part of figures ranging from George Eliot (Mary Ann Evans) to James Baldwin. Hempton says of Baldwin, for example, that while he acknowledged "the importance of evangelicalism in shaping American black identity" of which he was part, "he also hated its manifold petty hypocrisies, its collaborationist instincts, and its propensity to avoid the tough issues in facing up to the realities of the black experience in America."[44] Hypocrisy is a recurring theme throughout the book[45] and casts a shadow on evangelicalism, which was predominately inerrantist in the years the book covers.

More recently Craig Keener, in his excellent study of historical Jesus scholarship, has mentioned the role hypocrisy played in justifying the atheism of his younger years. Now an acknowledged evangelical scholar teaching at a seminary[46] holding to a high (though not explicitly inerrantist) view of Scripture, he writes the following about his past convictions:

> When I was an atheist . . . one of my central . . . objections to believing anything about Jesus was that eighty percent of people in my country [the United States] claimed to be his followers, yet most of them apparently lived as if it made no difference for their lives. . . . Much of western Christendom does not proceed as if the Jesus of the Gospels is alive and continues to reign in his church. . . . I concluded that if Christians did not really believe in Jesus, there was surely no reason for myself to do so.[47]

Such testimonies could be multiplied. They remind us that there is a close relation between the plausibility of doctrines and the integrity of those who hold and advocate those doctrines. Resistance

43. David Hempton, *Evangelical Disenchantment: Nine Portraits of Faith and Doubt* (New Haven, CT: Yale University Press, 2008).
44. Ibid., 17.
45. See the index in ibid., 229, for reference to about a dozen passages.
46. I.e., Palmer Theological Seminary of Eastern University.
47. Craig Keener, *The Historical Jesus of the Gospels* (Grand Rapids: Eerdmans, 2009), 384–85.

to inerrancy claims may relate to how we inerrantists fail to live what we confess. As the Cape Town Commitment affirms in its section on Scripture:

> We confess that we easily claim to love the Bible without loving the life it teaches—the life of costly practical obedience to God through Christ. Yet "nothing commends the gospel more eloquently than a transformed life, and nothing brings it into disrepute so much as personal inconsistency."[48]

## Advocacy of Inerrancy with a Coercive Spirit

John Piper writes recently of visiting a church on vacation where the preacher "spent his whole sermon hammering on people to come to the midweek meetings on Wednesday nights! And hammering on them to give money!"[49] Piper speaks then of biblical motivation, the knowledge that it is more blessed to give than to receive, and the Pauline exhortation of the joy of giving. Piper counsels:

> Don't try to manipulate people. Don't try to coerce people and make them do things. It has to come from inside, from their hearts. And that means they need knowledge that awakens love. People's affections are changed by what they know. Knowledge itself is, of course, not sufficient, as we have seen (the Devil has plenty). But it is necessary. The Holy Spirit uses it to awaken new desires and new wonders and joys. That is how God is exalted in changed behaviors.[50]

There is a valuable application here for the inerrancy doctrine. Biblical literacy has taken a hit in many circles in recent decades. Even people who want to believe all of the Bible to the fullest pos-

48. Cape Town Commitment, accessed June 1, 2011, http://www.lausanne.org/ctcommitment#p1-6. The words in quotation marks are from the Manila Manifesto.

49. John Piper and D. A. Carson, *The Pastor as Scholar and the Scholar as Pastor* (Wheaton, IL: Crossway, 2011), 60.

50. Ibid., 60–61.

sible extent may be deficient in knowledge of what the Bible says. Add to this the fact, as many of us can attest, that even if we possess sound knowledge of the Bible, it is no easy thing to be able to defend the Bible's truth at points where it is questioned. Informed advocacy of inerrancy typically requires years of study, often knowledge of ancient languages, and not seldom graduate degrees or the equivalent. Extensive pastoral or academic teaching experience is also helpful. All of these things take time, commitment, sacrifice, and the blessing of God.

We go astray when we bind people's consciences to convictions that they have not had sufficient opportunity to embrace personally in an informed way. We may actually damage people's moral and emotional health by pressuring them to assent to a doctrine like inerrancy before they have an adequate grasp of what this means. WCF 3.8 states regarding one of our key doctrines, "The doctrine of this high mystery of predestination is to be handled with special prudence and care" to avoid unintended outcomes like lack of assurance. This is surely no less true for the doctrine of Scripture from which the doctrine of predestination is derived.

This means, among much else, that pastors and scholars serving the church must be concerned for more than *that* people affirm inerrancy as a doctrinal proposition. Leaders must assume full responsibility for the hard work of teaching God's people, the demanding call to love God's people, the mysterious labor of motivating God's people, and the humbling task of living with integrity alongside and before God's people in such a way that the truth about the Bible is not hampered by a cavalier representation of it. Paul's cry, "Who is adequate for these things?" (2 Cor. 2:16) reverberates here. We are dependent on God's grace for our own minds and consciences to be clear about the Bible's truth and authority. This is doubly true for those we lead, including upcoming generations.

## CONCLUSION

It has been many years since Harry Emerson Fosdick preached his famous sermon "Shall the Fundamentalists Win?" in 1922.[51] Given the way he defined fundamentalists in that sermon—as hateful and bitterly intolerant—we can sympathize with his insistence that they deserve to be opposed. He left room for conservatives who were not fundamentalists to be part of the worshiping, inquiring, tolerant church he envisioned. Probably this is where we would like to place ourselves, not among "fighting fundies" in the worst sense. But Fosdick also attacked the doctrine of inerrancy. In hindsight, it is clear that whatever the outcomes for the partisan conflicts and leading personalities at that time, the Ritschlian liberalism informing Fosdick and his allies paid a high price for its decision to abandon the church's historic view of Scripture. Today this low view of Scripture is associated with a mainline that casts a pale shadow compared to its hegemony in the mid-twentieth century. J. Gresham Machen was right that liberalism was in key respects at best a cultural adaptation of some parts of the Christian tradition.[52] It was not the faith delivered once for all to the saints but a betrayal as serious as any committed by "fundamentalists."

Internationally God has since blessed the world with a wave of at least surface appropriation of the gospel message understood in terms largely amenable to inerrantist conviction and often explicitly inerrantist. We in the PCA do not need to be defensive about our high view of Scripture. For decades now some of our brightest and best young folk have committed to gospel ministry under inerrantist auspices and have become exemplary teaching pastors and church planters and missionaries. Hundreds have earned PhDs and are in a position to meet skeptical challenges in ways unthinkable just a few decades ago. For example, one can place alongside Bart Ehrman's

51. Harry Emerson Fosdick, "Shall the Fundamentalists Win?" accessed June 1, 2022, http://historymatters.gmu.edu/d/5070/.

52. See J. Gresham Machen, *Christianity and Liberalism* (1923; repr., Grand Rapids: Eerdmans, 2009).

recent attack on the Bible entitled *Forged*[53] the excellent studies by Charles Hill (from Reformed Theological Seminary in Orlando), *Who Chose the Gospels? Probing the Great Gospel Conspiracy*,[54] and that by Andreas Köstenberger (a Baptist scholar) and Michael Kruger (from Reformed Seminary in Charlotte) entitled *The Heresy of Orthodoxy*,[55] a pair of books that join a number of others in taking the wind out of Ehrman's sails. Or on another issue, one notes the important study by my colleague C. John Collins on matters pertaining to Adam and Eve.[56] There are many reasons to be confident that a high view of Scripture, the church's historic view of inerrancy, has a bright future.

I glimpsed this future last September in a church I have served in recent years. The prayer ministry leader, Jewish by birth but now Christian by faith, sent out an e-mail. We were to pray for Ted (not his real name) and his two boys, as Ted's wife and the boys' mother had just died of cancer. The e-mail said, "Pray that each clings tightly to the promises of Christ, that they trust HIM with their lives, have joy in their salvation, believe not just in Him but believe every thing He has said in His Word."[57] We often hear it said that we worship God and not a book. This servant of the church reminded us that there is the converse need to lay hold of "every thing He has said in His Word," apart from which personal relationship with God through a Christ of biblical proportions is imperiled. This is Scripture-centered faith that has a future in God's hands.

Yet there are storm clouds visible. Some of the sons and daughters of evangelicalism, and yes their fathers and mothers too, are adopting views analogous to those of Fosdick long ago.

---

53. Bart D. Ehrman, *Forged: Writing in the Name of God—Why the Bible's Authors Are Not Who We Think They Are* (New York: HarperOne, 2011).

54. Charles E. Hill, *Who Chose the Gospels? Probing the Great Gospel Conspiracy* (Oxford: Oxford University Press, 2010).

55. Andreas J. Köstenberger and Michael J. Kruger, *The Heresy of Orthodoxy: How Contemporary Culture's Fascination with Diversity Has Reshaped Our Understanding of Early Christianity* (Wheaton, IL: Crossway, 2010).

56. C. John Collins, *Did Adam and Eve Really Exist? Who They Were and Why You Should Care* (Wheaton, IL: Crossway, 2011).

57. Personal correspondence.

The hundreds of millions of new believers in the global South are not yet always well tethered to a recognizable, proven, doctrinally rich Christian confession. Both in the United States and abroad, political and religious and demographic and economic forces are arrayed against the church of God in ways that are resulting in martyrdoms on a numeric scale never seen before in the history of the church.[58] God alone knows what our future holds and whether Christian courage will rise to the challenges or evaporate. We hear Jesus' haunting question, "When the Son of Man comes, will he find faith on earth?" (Luke 18:8). We do know that we are dependent on God's gracious working to uphold the truths he has entrusted to us. Nowhere is this truer than with regard to the doctrine of biblical inerrancy.

---

58. Note the significant role martyrdoms play in, e.g., Mark Noll and Carolyn Nystrom, *Clouds of Witnesses: Christian Voices from Africa and Asia* (Downers Grove, IL: InterVarsity Press, 2011).

# 5

# God and Language[1]

## VERN S. POYTHRESS

CAN GOD SPEAK TO US? Does he? The twenty-first century intellectual environments in the Western world promote suspicions about language. Unbelievers sometimes reason that language is *merely* human, and therefore incapable of expressing the nature of the divine or the transcendent. They would say that we are just talking to ourselves, and everything we say about the transcendent realm falls short of truth.

When we read the Bible, we know better. The Bible is the Word of God, God's own speech to us. God does speak to us, and he speaks effectively.

We recognize the character of the Bible because the Holy Spirit has opened our eyes to realize that it is God who speaks.[2] But can

---

1. This article is a summary of some of the ideas from Vern S. Poythress, *In the Beginning Was the Word: Language—A God-Centered Approach* (Wheaton, IL: Crossway, 2009).

2. WCF 1.5 expresses it well: "We may be moved and induced by the testimony of the Church to an high and reverent esteem of the Holy Scripture. And the heavenliness

we respond directly to the arguments of those who are skeptical? In the long run, we need to appropriate what the Bible has to say about language if we are to respond to unbelievers and to protect ourselves and other believers from the inroads of skeptical thinking about language.

## LANGUAGE AND THE TRINITY

We can begin with John 1:1: "In the beginning was the Word, and the Word was with God, and the Word was God." In this context, "the Word" is a designation for the second person of the Trinity, but it also naturally suggests an association with language. But what is John 1:1 actually saying? The phrase *in the beginning*, as well as the continuation in John 1:2–4, alludes to Genesis 1: "In the beginning, God created the heavens and the earth" (Gen. 1:1).

The rest of Genesis 1 indicates that God performed his creative work by speaking:

> And *God said*, "Let there be light," and there was light. (Gen. 1:3)[3]
> And *God said*, "Let there be an expanse in the midst of the waters."
> (Gen. 1:6)
> And *God said*, "Let the waters under the heavens be gathered
> together into one place." (Gen. 1:9)

Psalm 33:6 sums up the work of creation:

> By the *word* of the LORD the heavens were made,
> and by the *breath of his mouth* all their host.

---

of the matter, the efficacy of the doctrine, the majesty of the style, the consent of all the parts, the scope of the whole (which is, to give all glory to God), the full discovery it makes of the only way of man's salvation, the many other incomparable excellencies, and the entire perfection thereof, are arguments whereby it doth abundantly evidence itself to be the Word of God: yet notwithstanding, our full persuasion and assurance of the infallible truth and divine authority thereof, is from *the inward work* of the Holy Spirit bearing witness by and with the Word in our hearts" (emphasis added).

3. Any italics within biblical quotations are my own addition.

In Genesis 1 God also addresses human beings in speech:

> And God blessed them. And *God said to them*, "Be fruitful and multiply and fill the earth and subdue it and have dominion over the fish of the sea and over the birds of the heavens and over every living thing that moves on the earth." (Gen. 1:28)

John 1:1, by alluding to this background, indicates that God's own Trinitarian nature lies behind the particular words that he spoke, both words to create the world and words addressed to human beings. Language runs deep. It is deeper and older than humanity. God spoke even before there were any human beings.

Genesis 1 records God's "Let there be light" speech and his other utterances in Hebrew so that we can understand them. But we do not know what language God used when he did his work of creation. In the utterances recorded in Genesis 1:3 and 6, God was not addressing man directly, but issuing commands for the world itself to come into being. We can have confidence that he did say, "Let there be light." But we do not know the details of the language in which he spoke. Since his utterances were not addressed to us, they may not have been in any *human* language. They are nevertheless accurately represented by the Hebrew rendering (and of course a later rendering in English or some other language into which the Hebrew can be translated). It is proper for us to say that God spoke, and that he used language, though we do not know all the details.

We may make analogous observations about John 1:1, which refers to God's *eternal* speaking. "In the beginning was the Word." The phrase *in the beginning* indicates that the Word always existed. This Word did not come into being at all, but always was. "The Word was God." So the expression "the Word" in John 1:1 cannot be simply identified with the words that God spoke to create the world in Genesis 1. This eternal Word comes before them all and remains forever. He always is. He is the *original* speech of God. We can see that John points out an analogy between the one eternal Word on the one hand and, on the other, the many particular words, that is, creational words, that God spoke according to Genesis 1. The many particular words rest ultimately on the involvement of the eternal Word in God's acts of creating the world:

> Yet for us there is one God, the Father, from whom are all things and for whom we exist, and one Lord, Jesus Christ, *through whom are all things* and through whom we exist. (1 Cor. 8:6)

> For by him [God the Son] all things were created. (Col. 1:16)

The eternal Word is the archetype, the original speech of God. The words God spoke to create are derivative, but still in harmony with this eternal Word, who was active in creation. The Holy Spirit was active as well, as we see from Genesis 1:2: "And the Spirit of God was hovering over the face of the waters." God's speech has the deepest possible roots, namely, in God himself, in his Trinitarian nature. The Trinity is a mystery to us. But this mystery guarantees that God's speech has depth. God says more and speaks more richly than what we are able to comprehend as creatures.

God's speech to human beings begins, as we noted, in Genesis 1:28–30. This speech, we conclude, is in harmony with the speeches he made to create the world. And it is in harmony with his eternal Word. It is empowered by the presence of the Spirit. Speech to human beings is therefore Trinitarian speech, and in harmony with the eternal speech of God. Interestingly, God speaks to human beings before there is any record of human beings speaking to one another. Human language is not *merely* human. It is not there *merely* as a practical, prosaic tool for human communication to other human beings. God is the originator. We should thank God for language; it is a gift. In addition, we should observe that this gift of language is designed by God for divine-human communication. God speaks to us in languages that he has already designed for that purpose. And we might say that such communication from God is more central even than communication among human beings, one to another. *God* addresses us. And, as we can see fairly soon in Genesis, human beings address God in return (Gen. 3:12).

## KNOWLEDGE THROUGH LANGUAGE

This biblical view of language differs radically from modern views, evolutionary or otherwise, that treat language as a mere accidental or convenient tool for this world. Many people who imbibe a modern worldview are suspicious of language. They say, "How can we presume to talk about God? How do we know that language will work effectively for such a purpose? Is God beyond language?"

This kind of skepticism can be answered most effectively only if we realize that non-Christians, with hearts in rebellion against God, have a different view of the world than Christians, whose hearts are regenerated by the Holy Spirit. Non-Christians are engaged in suppressing the truth about God (Rom. 1:18–23). Among other things, they suppress the revelation of God in the very texture of language. Language derives from God, yes, from God in his Trinitarian character. It is a constant witness to him. And it is a vehicle through which he speaks. God as master of language can speak just as he pleases. Language is no inhibition for him. Moreover, it does take God speaking for us to know him. Knowledge that we claim to have about God is not true knowledge if it is merely the invention of our own minds or of our own would-be autonomous speech about God. We need to attend to God as he speaks to us in the Bible. Through the work of the Spirit he overcomes, among those whom he draws to himself, the suppression of the truth that Romans 1 delineates. Through the Spirit he creates receptive hearts so that we can hear what he says, and we know him (2 Cor. 4:4–6).

The Bible speaks boldly about the fact that we can know God through what he says:

> "And this is eternal life, that they *know* you the only true God, and Jesus Christ whom you have sent." (John 17:3)

"I have manifested your name to the people whom you gave me out of the world. Yours they were, and you gave them to me, and they have kept *your word*. Now they know that everything that you have given me is from you. For I have given them *the words* that you gave me, and they have received them and have come to know in truth that I came from you; and they have believed that you sent me." (John 17:6–8)

The words Jesus speaks originate from the communion among the persons of the Trinity. Those words result in knowledge of God among those whom "you gave . . . to me" (John 17:6).

The Chicago Statement on Biblical Inerrancy by the International Council on Biblical Inerrancy sums it up:

We affirm that God who made mankind in His image has used language as a means of revelation.

We deny that human language is so limited by our creatureliness that it is rendered inadequate as a vehicle for divine revelation. We further deny that the corruption of human culture and language through sin has thwarted God's work of inspiration.[4]

We may now consider how a biblical view of language affects some particular issues about language and meaning.

## METAPHOR AND ANALOGY

First, what about metaphor and analogy? We call God "Father." This use of the word *Father* is analogous to, rather than identical with, the use of the word for human fathers. Does the use of analogy destroy the truth of what is being said? A non-Christian view of language might claim that it does. According to such a view, the only "true truth" is literal, scientific statement

4. "The Chicago Statement on Biblical Inerrancy," International Council on Biblical Inerrancy, 1978, Article IV, accessed May 24, 2011, http://www.alliancenet.org /partner/Article_Display_Page/0,,PTID307086_CHID750054_CIID2094584,00.html.

about facts. Everything else is a kind of improper stretching of language.

But this view is at odds with the Bible's view of language. Language as a gift from God has the capability for metaphor and analogy built into it by God. We can see this capability by considering the language for "father." The original Father is God the Father in relation to his Son. God makes man in his image, and then we see that Adam becomes the first human father in analogy with the pattern when God created Adam:

> When God created man, he made him in the likeness of God. Male and female he created them, and he blessed them and named them Man when they were created. When Adam had lived 130 years, he fathered a son *in his own likeness, after his image*, and named him Seth. (Gen. 5:2–3)

The language about "likeness" and "image" in Genesis 5:3 obviously picks up on similar language describing God's creation of man in Genesis 1:26. But now it is used to describe Adam fathering a son. The creation of man in the image of God gives a foundation for acts on the part of man that are analogical to the original acts of God.

Moreover, the language about "image of God" has an even deeper basis. We find in Colossians 1:15 that Christ is called "the image of the invisible God." Christ is the original image. The creation of man in Genesis 1 imitates this original imaging. Christ is being described in his role as Creator, so he is the *divine* image. We as creatures are creaturely images. The two are not identical. But they are analogous. God designs us to know by analogy with his knowledge. We speak by analogy with his speech (see Gen. 2:19–20). But the original analogy is divine rather than human: Christ is the image of God, and as such shows the character of the Father. He is the archetype for analogies that God ordains within this world. So God has in his wisdom built analogy into the world itself. And accordingly it is built into language. In fact, God's language governing the world specifies all analogies.

99

Thus analogy is not alien to language. It is built in. When rightly used, it expresses truth. We do know God the Father through the revelation of the Son in his words, as John 17 has indicated. We know what it means for him to be our Father through the Spirit's teaching (Rom. 8:15–17).

## HISTORY AND INTERPRETATION

A second skeptical strain within modern worldviews concerns history and reports of events in history. Can a report in language be faithful to what actually happened? Once again, non-Christian worldviews can interfere with a proper conception of the function of language. These views obscure the character of reports about events. In non-Christian thinking, it may be claimed that the events have meaning tacked onto them by human narration. The events have no meaning until human beings narrate them. And then, since there are multiple possible narrations, the meaning belongs to each human interpreter rather than to the event itself. All historical reporting is "biased" by the input from a human reporter.

By contrast, in a Christian worldview we know that God has a plan for history. His plan precedes the events. The events have purpose and meaning in the mind of God even *before* they take place. This meaning is infinite, since it coheres with God's entire purpose for the whole of history. Our human minds are not infinite, but we are made in the image of God. Made in God's image, we can access "true truth" about events as God reveals truths that are in his mind, either through special revelation in biblical accounts of events, or through general revelation, as we ourselves observe events or hear the reports of other fallible interpreters. Fallibility does not mean universal skepticism. God has made a world in which our minds are in fundamental coherence with the world, because God has made both our minds and the world after the pattern of his will. We can really know, though we know finitely.

Because God's mind is always richer than our knowledge, we can also account for why there may be more than one true account of the same event. All true accounts given to human beings are *partial* and selective, which, it is worth emphasizing, does not make them less than true. We are constantly having to oppose the non-Christian view of knowledge, which often insists that unless we know everything (by autonomous mastery), we can know nothing. The Gospels are a good example of rich accounts of events. The Gospels differ in their selectivity at some points, but each account expresses the mind of God. All the accounts together are in harmony and express more of the mind of God than we would access through only one account.

We can of course say that Matthew, Mark, Luke, and John, as human authors, are each giving his own "interpretation" of the events of the life of Jesus. But such interpretation is not *falsification*. Interpretation, especially when guided by the Spirit who inspired the Evangelists, draws out and re-expresses aspects of the purpose and meaning that God had in the events *from the beginning*. The human authors are not "creating" meaning, but expressing God's meaning, meaning that he already had. The events have always had meaning; there are no "bare" events with no meaning, because God controls all of history.

We can see this principle working in an obvious way with respect to the crucifixion and the resurrection of Christ. Old Testament symbols and prophecies lay out beforehand aspects of the meaning of the crucifixion and the resurrection. Jesus predicts these events and comments on their meaning beforehand (e.g., Mark 10:45). The Evangelists, inspired by the Spirit of Christ, then re-express the meaning after the events are accomplished. Both the differences among the Gospels and their commonalities are meanings known by God before the foundation of the world, and now expressed to us in time through the process of inspiration. God is speaking his meanings, which are *definitive* for the events.

101

## STABILITY OF MEANING

A non-Christian worldview may also create difficulties with respect to stability of meaning. On the one hand, non-Christians secretly aspire to be gods. They want to be the ultimate masters of meaning. So any flexibility in the range of meaning of a word or a sentence threatens to overthrow their mastery. They do not merely want stability, such as is guaranteed by the faithfulness of God to his own meanings, but godlike mastery. So they may overreach in claims about their understanding of this or that text of Scripture.

But in the cultures of the West today, people have reacted to this rationalistic extreme by going into postmodern irrationalism. A non-Christian worldview of this type admits that it falls short of absolute mastery. It then goes to the opposite extreme of ambiguity. Words, it might be claimed, may mean almost anything. And sentences may be reinterpreted indefinitely, with no visible boundaries for the endeavor. What do we say in response?

We need to avoid merely answering a non-Christian on his own terms. We must think biblically. To begin with, God's standards give us obligations. We have moral responsibility, which includes a responsibility to respect meanings from people made in the image of God. Above all, we respect meanings coming from God's own mouth, that is, the meanings in Scripture. The moral standards of God, which are absolute, give us reason for rejecting manipulative or fanciful interpretations, whereas an unbeliever, who cannot admit to absolutes, may feel free to multiply interpretations without limit.

God also provides contexts that eliminate many "theoretical ambiguities." The contexts—including the larger literary context of a biblical book, the context of the full canon of Scripture, the context of the human author, his purposes, his situation in history, and so on—all come to bear and enable us to discern that a word or a sentence is used in one way rather than another that would theoretically be possible in other circumstances. We trust God who controls all contexts, and enables us to receive his word with understanding.

We may take a particular example. Exodus 13:21 says,

> The LORD went before them by day in a pillar of cloud to lead them along the way, and by night in a pillar of fire to give them *light*, that they might travel by day and by night.

What is the meaning of the word *light*? The context of guidance through the wilderness indicates that a physical light is in view, coming from the supernatural phenomenon of the pillar of fire.

Now compare this use of *light* in Exodus to John 8:12. Jesus says, "I am the *light* of the world." The context, in which Jesus is talking about himself, and the larger context of the Gospel of John, where "light" is a repeated theme, indicate that the verse is talking about Jesus' role as revealer of God the Father, and by implication his role as guide to redemption and to eternal life. We can also see that the passage in Exodus and the passage in John 8:12 are related by analogy. In Exodus God used the physical light for physical guidance, intending it as a symbol for the larger role that he had in guiding the people spiritually and morally. The word *light* when viewed apart from any context whatsoever has the capability of designating physical light, moral light, spiritual light of revelation, blinding light, and so on. The contexts enable us to appreciate what meaning belongs to a particular occurrence. And the context of the whole of the canon can enable us to appreciate relationships between analogous meanings, such as the relation between Exodus and John 8:12.

We do understand. We understand truly. But we do not understand *comprehensively*, that is, in the way that only God can understand. When Jesus says that he is the light of the world, he makes a stupendous claim that we do not fathom completely. His statement is, among other things, one of the "I am" sayings in John. He also says, "I am the bread of life" (John 6:35); "I am the good shepherd" (John 10:11); "I am the resurrection and the life" (John 11:25); "I am the true vine" (John 15:1). We suspect that all these statements resonate with the "I am" in John 8:58, where Jesus claims to be eternally existent and uses a form of speech that expresses the meaning of the Tetragrammaton (the "I am" of Ex. 3:14).

God is light (1 John 1:5). The ultimate anchorage for the word *light* is in God himself, who is light. God by his own character and faithfulness gives ultimate stability to meaning in this world. He shows himself to us in speech, including speech about light. He makes definite claims. Only God knows himself perfectly and exhaustively. But we do not need to be God in order to know him truly by receiving his speech in the Son through the power of the Holy Spirit.

## THE ONE AND THE MANY

Still another difficulty arises in a non-Christian approach to language. How can words like *horse* apply to a multitude of horses? How do we know what we are talking about? The difficulty can be generalized to apply not only to language but also to the world about which we speak. Why are there many horses with one common pattern, belonging to one species? This difficulty is called the problem of the one and the many. How does the one, namely, the general category of horse, relate to the many, namely, the many horses?

Darwinian naturalism thinks it has an answer in unguided Darwinian evolution. Evolution produces both a species and the members of the species. But Darwinian naturalism does not give us an answer to the deeper difficulty: why is there order at all? Naturalism depends on the concept of scientific law, which provides a foundation for the unity of the species and the unity of species behavior. Why does law have the character of unity (a single law) and diversity (applying to many individual instances)? And why does human language express this unity and diversity? Is language adequate to the world?

A Christian view of language, as usual, traces meanings back to God. It is God who has established both the one and the many in the world by his speech. And his speech coheres with himself. God is one God in three persons. God himself offers us the ultimate instance of one and many. Out of this one and many in God, he creates a world with one and many according to the specifications of his word of command. God's language specifies one and many. Human language, which reflects God's language, also is capable of interacting with one and many. That is why we have one word, *horse*, that we can use to designate many horses as well as the species horse.

By contrast, modern non-Christian worldviews are typically *nominalistic*. Words are names ("nominal") that we humans invent (out of thin air?) to produce unity. Is the unity then a humanly imposed illusion? Immanuel Kant came near to this idea by arguing that the categories of time, space, and causality were imposed on phenomena by the human mind. In this view, human beings virtually "create" the world of experience. But this kind of view threatens a radical subjectivism. And once we lose the conviction that all human minds are basically the same, we can arrive at a postmodern skepticism about both the unity of meaning and knowledge. Meaning and so-called "knowledge" are alleged to be "created" by human societies by their conventions. And differences among different societies threaten the unity of meaning and knowledge for humanity as a whole.

According a biblical worldview, God has created the world and human beings. He has given us as human beings language in analogy with his language specifying the one and many in the world. The harmony in God's plan leads to a basic harmony among language, human beings, and the world—in which radical skepticism has no place.

## CONCLUSION

In sum, assumptions about language do have an influence when people consider the claims of Scripture. Many modern thinkers assume that human language is *merely* human, merely a pragmatic tool for managing a world of bare or "brute" facts, facts with no intrinsic grounding in language. The Bible presents us with a very different picture. God made the world and governs it by the wisdom of his providence. Moreover, he governs by *speaking*. The world in its overall structure and in the details of its history is the product of language—God's language. Human beings are creatures, not God. But we are made in the image of God, and the language that God has given us as a gift is designed by God. So it matches both the world and the nature of God as he reveals himself when he speaks in language.

This biblical conception of language provides responses to various objections and skeptical theories about language. "God-talk," language about God, is not intrinsically problematic. It is not a "stretching" of language beyond its design, but a use according to its design. People can of course use language to express heretical or blasphemous thoughts about God. But this is a difficulty created by the fall and by sin, not a difficulty intrinsic to the metaphysical character of language as given by God.

Skeptics also doubt whether historical events can be adequately described in language, whether language provides stable meanings, and whether language is problematic because of the problem of the one and the many. A biblical basis for understanding language provides coherent responses to these objections. The Bible is still the Word of God, and still expresses truth about God, truth about history, truth about meaning, and truth about the one and the many. In these and other questions, we are not supposed to follow in our thinking the way of the world, but the way of Christ, as he has taught us by speaking in Scripture (2 Cor. 10:5).

# 6

## N. T. Wright and the
## Authority of Scripture

### JOHN M. FRAME

N. T. WRIGHT is one of the best known among New Testament scholars today. He has been a prolific author of both scholarly and popular works. Many of his popular writings are published under the less formal name Tom Wright. His published output is astounding; I stopped counting at fifty books, and of course he has also produced a huge number of articles, published sermons, audio lectures, and multi-media presentations. He was also Bishop of Durham in the Church of England for a number of years, but he is presently a research professor at the University of St. Andrews in Scotland.

Wright is best known for his development of the so-called "New Perspective on Paul," advocated originally by E. P. Sanders and James D. G. Dunn. Wright's view of Paul has led him into controversy, especially concerning the doctrine of justification. But beyond this controversy, Wright is considered conservative. He believes that the story recorded in Scripture is substantially historical, and he has no bias against the supernatural as such. Indeed, he has published a significant defense of the resurrection of Jesus, setting forth its historicity, centrality, and saving power.[1] He has little regard for the skeptical trends in modern biblical scholarship, such as the famous Jesus Seminar.

I am especially enthusiastic about Wright's understanding of the broad narrative structure of Scripture. For Wright, the Bible is the story of the coming of God's kingdom in power, a political event that from its beginning challenged the Roman Empire. He is, therefore, an opponent of privatized religion, an advocate of a Christian faith that seeks with God's help to bring all things subject to Christ. He recognizes the centrality of the *Lordship* of Christ.

## A *DOCTRINE* OF SCRIPTURE?

Wright, then, has excellent insight into the content of Scripture and has defended effectively the truth of Scripture. But what does he say about the nature of Scripture? What is his *doctrine* of the Bible?

Wright does not put much emphasis on the doctrinal question. He wants to avoid emphasizing general questions about the Bible's nature, its authority, infallibility, and inerrancy, so that he can focus on the content of Scripture. We'll see why a bit later. But in fact he does address the theological doctrine of Scripture, chiefly in three places. First, in a 1989 lecture called "How Can the Bible Be Authoritative?" published in *Vox Evangelica* in 1991.[2] Second, in a 2005 book titled *The Last Word: Scripture and the Authority of God*.[3]

---

1. N. T. Wright, *The Resurrection of the Son of God*, vol. 3 of *Christian Origins and the Question of God* (Minneapolis: Fortress Press, 2003).

2. N. T. Wright, "How Can the Bible Be Authoritative?" *VE* 21 (1991): 7–32. Available online at http://www.ntwrightpage.com/Wright_Bible_Authoritative.htm.

3. N. T. Wright, *The Last Word: Scripture and the Authority of God* (San Francisco: HarperSanFrancisco, 2005). Published in the United Kingdom as *Scripture and the Authority of God*. Hereafter *LW*.

Besides the title and the subtitle of this book, there is a significant sub-subtitle: "Beyond the Bible Wars to a New Understanding of the Authority of Scripture." I reviewed this book, and you can find the review as an Appendix to my book *The Doctrine of the Word of God*.[4] Third, Wright's apologetic work, *Simply Christian: Why Christianity Makes Sense*,[5] discusses the nature of Scripture in a number of places. As is implicit in the title, intentionally reminiscent of C. S. Lewis's *Mere Christianity*, this book is a popular rather than academic text. *The Last Word* is a bit more technical, directed, I believe, to church leaders, but not to the academy as such.

These writings will be disappointing if the reader is looking for a traditional systematic account of the doctrine of the Word of God, revelation, and Scripture.[6] But there are a number of ideas that Wright does want to convey. I think the best way to proceed is for me to list these ideas one by one with some of my own comments.

## THE AUTHORITY OF SCRIPTURE IS THE AUTHORITY OF GOD EXPRESSED THROUGH SCRIPTURE

In *The Last Word*, Wright says that the "central claim of this book" is that the phrase *authority of Scripture* can make Christian sense only if it is a shorthand for "the authority of the triune God, exercised somehow *through* Scripture."[7] I think that most theologians of all traditions would agree with this statement. To conservative evangelicals, the most important thing about the Bible is indeed

4. John M. Frame, *The Doctrine of the Word of God* (Phillipsburg, NJ: P&R Publishing, 2010).

5. N. T. Wright, *Simply Christian: Why Christianity Makes Sense* (San Francisco: HarperSanFrancisco, 2006). Hereafter *SC*.

6. In *VE* he says, "One might even say, in one (admittedly limited) sense, that there is no biblical doctrine of the authority of the Bible." But later in the article he says, "But, according to Paul in Romans 15 and elsewhere, the Bible is itself a key part of God's plan. It is not merely a divinely given commentary on the way salvation works (or whatever); the Bible is part of the means by which he puts his purposes of judgement and salvation to work."

7. *LW*, 23; cf. 116; Wright, *SC*, 185; *VE*.

its relation to God, in the sense that it is God's Word and therefore speaks with God's own authority. That evangelical conviction can be formulated by means of Wright's statement.

On the other hand, Wright's statement seems intended to make a *distinction* between God's authority and Scripture as its instrument. The little word "somehow" enlarges the distance between God and Scripture. Certainly there are distinctions between God and Scripture, even for conservative evangelicals, but some kinds of distinctions are controversial.

Barth, for example, has used this kind of formulation to suggest that only God speaks literal words of God, and the Bible, though a derivative of God's authority, does not itself speak with divine authority. It is a witness or instrument of divine revelation, but it is not itself divine revelation. So Barth would agree with Wright that the authority of Scripture is the authority of God expressed through Scripture, but his view is very different from that of evangelical theologians. So it becomes important to understand what kind of differences between Scripture and God Wright has in mind.

As we shall see, Wright's view is not Barthian, but he does not assert the equation between God's words and the Bible's that is typical of evangelical accounts. He wants to indicate, I think, that the relationship between Scripture and God is more complicated, more problematic, than evangelicals, especially American evangelicals, have thought it to be. It is a "somehow" relationship. Hopefully we shall gain some clarity on this issue as we look at his further assertions.

## SCRIPTURE IS NARRATIVE

Wright gives us some insight as to the sorts of problems he wrestles with in regard to biblical authority, when he asks what kind of book Scripture is. In *The Last Word*, he says,

The Bible itself, as a whole and in most of its parts, is not the sort of thing that many people envisage today when they hear the word "authority."

It is not, for a start, a list of rules, though it contains many commandments of various sorts and in various contexts. Nor is it a compendium of true doctrines, though of course many parts of the Bible declare great truths about God, Jesus, the world and ourselves in no uncertain terms. Most of its constituent parts, and all of it when put together . . . can best be described as a *story.*[8]

The question is, How can a story be authoritative? If the commanding officer walks into the barrack-room and begins "Once upon a time," the soldiers are likely to be puzzled. . . . At first sight, what we think of as "authority" and what we know as "story" do not readily fit together.[9]

Now many theologians today identify Scripture as a story or narrative. But I think that identification oversimplifies the nature of Scripture, even as a literary description. Certainly there is a great deal of historical narrative in Scripture, what we call redemptive history, the story of creation, fall, and redemption. But much of Scripture is not narrative, but law, poetry, wisdom, letters, apocalyptic. It can be argued that these other literary forms depend on the narrative, but they should not be reduced to narrative.

I have found more persuasive Meredith Kline's contention[10] that the *combination* of these literary forms in Scripture suggests that the best way to characterize Scripture as a whole is not "narrative," but "covenant." Covenant in this sense refers to a complex literary form represented in ancient near eastern suzerainty treaties. The biblical term *covenant* often describes this sort of

8. *LW*, 25–26. Nor, he says later, should Scripture be described primarily as revelation, or as a devotional manual (30–34). He opposes the idea that Scripture is a *lectio divina* in *LW*, 64, though in *SC*, 188, he does endorse that use of Scripture.

9. *LW*, 26.

10. Meredith G. Kline, *The Structure of Biblical Authority* (Grand Rapids: Eerdmans, 1972). My own understanding of the content of Scripture follows his to an extent. See my *Doctrine of the Word of God*, 145–62.

treaty, particularly treaties between God and people like Noah, Abraham, Moses, and David.[11] These treaties included historical narrative, but also law, sanctions, and administrative matters. In the ancient world, the great king would command the lesser king to reverence the treaty document, the covenant, between the two parties, to put it in a holy place, and to hear it over and over again. In Israel, God ordered the people to put the Decalogue and the various additions to it in the holiest place of the tabernacle and later the temple. The covenant document was their supreme constitution. It is narrative, but not only narrative. It is, like the US Constitution, the highest law of the land for God's people. This model, far better than Wright's, shows how Scripture functions as authority for God's people.

To some extent the search for a general literary description of Scripture is futile. Since Scripture is God's Word, it is unique, *sui generis*. But if we need a general term for the literary nature of Scripture, we should describe it as *covenant*, God's treaty with us, the constitution of the people of God. To say this is not to disparage the narrative. Certainly, in a sense, all the content of the Bible depends on that narrative. But Scripture is not *only* narrative.

Whether Kline is right or not about the general content of Scripture, his proposal should open us to see that Scripture contains a rich variety of literary genres, each of which conveys to us a form of authority. Narratives are to be believed, commandments to be obeyed, psalms to be taken to heart, wisdom to be cultivated in our hearts, apocalyptic to arouse our amazement, letters to play the many functions that letters play in our experience.

11. These treaties were documents that a greater king would impose upon a lesser king, including the name of the great king, the "historical prologue," indicating the past relationships of the two parties, laws of various kinds, then sanctions: benefits for obeying and curses for disobeying, and finally, administrative matters. Kline argued that the elements of these treaties correspond to the elements of biblical covenants such as the Decalogue and that the elements of the biblical canon reflect this structure. If Kline is right, the narrative of Scripture is "historical prologue," a prelude to the laws, the sanctions, and the administration of God's kingdom.

## The Authority of Scripture Is the Application of Its Story

Wright acknowledges this complexity in the material quoted above. But when he formulates the question of the nature of biblical authority, as we have seen, he thinks it reduces entirely to the question of how a narrative or story can have authority. To answer this question, he thinks, is like answering the question of how a commanding officer can give orders that begin "once upon a time."

He answers that question as follows:

> For a start, the commanding officer might well need to brief the soldiers about what has been going on over the past few weeks, so that they will understand the sensitivities and internal dynamics of the peace-keeping task they are now to undertake. The narrative will bring them up to date; now it will be their task to act out the next chapter in the ongoing saga.[12]

Other examples:

> A familiar story told with a new twist in the tail jolts people into thinking differently about themselves and the world. A story told with pathos, humor or drama opens the imagination and invites readers and hearers to imagine themselves in similar situations, offering new insights about God and human beings which enable them then to order their own lives more wisely.[13]

In the first example, the narrative informs the soldiers of events relevant to their military task. In the second, it motivates imaginations and gives insight. Now as we saw, Wright earlier said that even though Scripture is not "a compendium of true doctrines" it does "declare great truths about God." It certainly seems to me, and I think Wright would agree, that these great truths could be

12. *LW*, 26.
13. Ibid., 27.

among the "new insights about God and human beings which enable them then to order their own lives more wisely." So it is certainly possible for the traditional concerns of systematic theology to be integrated into Wright's narrative theology. The same certainly can be said for the traditional concerns of Christian morality. So Wright's model, though I prefer a different one as I have said, is flexible enough to incorporate most, if not all, of our traditional uses of the Bible. It does not require a radical change as might be expected from Wright's sub-subtitle, "a new understanding of the authority of Scripture."

Traditional theology and ethics have always understood, to a greater or lesser degree, that narrative is important in Scripture. The narrative is the good news that God has saved his people through his actions in history. There is no such gospel in Hinduism, or Buddhism, or in Islam. Traditional Christian theology explains these events and, I should add, the worldview they presuppose. Christian ethics tells us not only what the God of the narrative expects of us, but also the new motivation for obedience that comes through the narrative. Wright's narrative emphasis may give a fresh impetus to these themes, but he has not told us anything here that we haven't known already. If he had denied that there were any "great truths about God" in Scripture, or that there are no ethical norms and motivations in Scripture, that Scripture is *only* narrative and nothing else, then he would have said something very original, radical, and peculiar. But he is, in the final analysis, a rather traditional Christian in his conception of the content of Scripture. My earlier suggestion that he broaden his concept of the content of Scripture beyond narrative to covenant would constitute a tweaking of his concept, not a fundamental change of it.

## SCRIPTURE IS POWER, NOT ONLY WORD

But Wright, seeking to establish the newness of his supposedly new understanding of biblical authority, often resorts to the idea that Scripture is not merely a text, but also a vehicle of the power of God. It not only says things; it does things as well. That is to say that the functions of Scripture are not only verbal, but also something more.

Wright speaks of God's authority as "his sovereign power accomplishing the renewal of all creation. Specific authority over human beings, notably the church, must be seen as part of that larger whole."[14] What role does Scripture play in this divine project?

> It is enormously important that we see the role of scripture not simply as being to provide *true information about*, or even an accurate running commentary upon, the work of God in salvation and new creation, but as taking an active part *within* that ongoing purpose. . . . Scripture is there to be a means of God's action in and through us—which will include, but go far beyond, the mere conveying of information.[15]

Here, Wright touches on the question of "propositional revelation" that in the 1940s and '50s was central in the debate between evangelicals and neoorthodox thinkers. The neoorthodox, like Barth and Brunner, thought that it was unworthy of God for us to imagine him conveying propositions, or items of information, to human beings. Evangelicals, on the other hand, insisted that much of Scripture, including its historical narrative, was informative, and so, propositional revelation was an obvious feature of Scripture. They conceded, in their best formulations, that Scripture contained not only items of information, but also commands, questions, poetic expressions, parables, wisdom sayings, and so on. But that was not enough for the neoorthodox, who thought that by renouncing propositional revelation entirely they could escape the whole idea of revelation as words in favor of some kind of nonverbal revelation that we may be inclined to call mystical.

14. Ibid., 29.
15. Ibid., 30.

Wright too wants to get beyond the idea of propositional revelation, though unlike the neoorthodox he does not want to deny
verbal revelation altogether. Still, he agrees with the neoorthodox
that biblical revelation is not only more than propositional revelation; it is more even than verbal revelation. Beyond words, it is a
power. The Word of God, he says, is "not . . . a synonym for the
written scriptures, but . . . a strange personal presence, creating,
judging, healing, recreating."[16] Wright also contends that "the early
Christians discovered that telling this story [the gospel] carried a
power which they regularly associated with the Spirit, but which
they often referred to simply as 'the word.'"[17]

In *Simply Christian*, he uses the metaphor that Scripture is a
kind of holy ground, a place where heaven and earth meet. This
is a frequent theme of the book. Wright presents three worldview
options: In Option One, there are writers (pantheists, in effect)
who identify heaven and earth so that they are indistinguish-
able. But there are others, he says (deists), who make heaven
and earth far apart so that God cannot get involved in earthly
history. This is Option Two. Scripture, he says, presents still
a third option: heaven and earth are distinct, but they often
come together so that we experience heaven, God's presence,
in history.[18]

So when he considers the nature of inspiration, Wright opposes
the "dictation" view, which he thinks comes out of an alternative
version of Option Two: heaven and earth are generally separated, but
God sometimes breaks through the division, "'zapping' the [bibli-
cal] writers with some kind of long-range linguistic thunderbolt."[19]
That is not a plausible view, he thinks, of the relationship between
God and the biblical writers. But he says,

16. Ibid., 38.
17. *SC*, 134. He refers also to the advance and growth of the "word" in Acts 4:31;
6:7; 12:24; 19:20; Rom. 10:8–9; Col. 1:5–6; 1 Thess. 2:13; see also Ps. 33:6.
18. I have made a very similar point in my own books, speaking of various views
of transcendence and immanence, rather than of heaven and earth.
19. *SC*, 181.

Once again Option Three comes to the rescue. Supposing scripture, like the sacraments, is one of the points where heaven and earth overlap and interlock? Like all other such places, this is mysterious. It doesn't mean that we can see at once what's going on. Indeed, it guarantees that we can't. But it does enable us to say some things that need to be said and that are otherwise difficult.

In particular, it enables us to say that the writers, compilers, editors, and even collectors of scripture were people who, with different personalities, styles, methods, and intentions, were nonetheless caught up in the strange purposes of the covenant God—purposes which included the communication, by writing, of his word.[20]

So Scripture is a sacred place, where heaven and earth meet, not just a book. It is a book, but more, something mysterious, something powerful, as we have seen.

Wright says that this is strange, and indeed it is. This is evidently what he means when he says that "somehow" God exerts his authority through Scripture. But like his emphasis on narrative it is not unprecedented in Protestant theology. The idea of the "power" of the Word has been part of Protestant thought since the Reformation, and the classical Reformers have referred to the same collection of biblical texts that Wright does here. The Word is "living and powerful," as Hebrew 4:12 says. It is "the power of God unto salvation" (Rom. 1:16). Indeed (wouldn't you know it?) there has been a debate between the Reformed and Lutheran camps as to *how* we should understand the relationship between the power of the Word and the power of the Spirit; but I digress. The idea of Scripture as a sacramental location of God's presence sounds more Catholic than Protestant, but Protestants too have drawn many parallels between the Word and the sacraments. The sacraments are visible words, and the sense in which God is present in the sacraments, for Protestants, is easily applicable to the Word.

20. Ibid.

So even Wright's mysterious talk about the Word as a power and as a sacramental location of God does not justify the notion that he is proposing a "new understanding of the authority of Scripture." Rather, Wright has reformulated and perhaps rediscovered ways of thinking about Scripture that are common in Protestant theological tradition. If he were to deny that revelation is also a written text, he would be departing from that tradition and joining the neoorthodox. But as we have seen, he does not do that.[21]

## GOD DOES SPEAK TO US BY WORD

To underscore this section title, I should point out that most of Wright's references to God's speech are in conventional linguistic terms, though, as we have seen, he sometimes describes divine communication as something more than language. We recall that for him the authority of Scripture is the authority of narrative; but narrative is a verbal form and propositional to boot. Although Wright stresses in context that the function of Scripture is to "energize" us for God's task, he rejects the notion that revelation is nonverbal. Of course, it is the *words* of Scripture, as we read, hear, and understand them, that energize us for God's task. Option Three, Wright says,

> enables us to speak about God the creator (the one we know supremely through the living Word, Jesus) being himself (so to speak) a wordsmith. Option Three enables us to insist that, though words are not the only thing God specializes in, they are a central part of his repertoire . . . he wants to communicate with and through [his people] verbally—in addition to, but also as a central point within, his many other ways of getting things said and done.
> The Bible is far more, in other words, than what some people used to say a generation or so ago: that it was simply the (or a)

21. Some readers may find it interesting and/or amusing that Wright has here uncovered what I have elsewhere referred to as a "covenantal triad": The authority of the Bible is by word (normative), power (situational), and by its sacramental nature as a dwelling place of God (existential).

"record of the revelation," as if God revealed himself by some quite other means and the Bible was simply what people wrote down to remind themselves of what had happened. The Bible offers itself, and has normally been treated in the church, as part of God's revelation, not simply a witness or echo of it.[22]

In *The Last Word*, he says that the existence of the Bible

> reminds us that the God Christians worship is characterized not least as a God who *speaks*, who communicates with his human creatures in words. . . . It means that the idea of reading a book to hear and know God is not far-fetched, but cognate with the nature of God himself.[23]

The bottom line, then, is that God speaks to his people in a very ordinary sense of "speaking," but that Scripture is more than that. Again, we find a clear correspondence between Wright's view and the traditional Protestant view of Scripture. So far we have seen nothing that looks like a "new understanding of the authority of Scripture."

## WE SHOULD NOT ASK WHETHER THE WHOLE TEXT OF SCRIPTURE IS TRUE

So far I have not differed very much with Wright, save some quibbles about his over-emphasis on the narrative character of Scripture. But there are some other matters about which I have more serious reservations with his formulation, particularly his statements about biblical inspiration, infallibility, and inerrancy.

In my review of *The Last Word*, I criticized Wright's understanding of biblical inspiration. He says it is "a shorthand way of talking about the belief that by his Spirit God guided the very

22. *SC*, 181–82.
23. *LW*, 34.

different writers and editors, so that the books they produced were the books God intended his people to have."[24] I replied,

> But the same can be said about the books in my library: that God moved writers, editors, publishers, et al., so that the books in my library are the ones God wants me to have. Nevertheless, there are some horrible books in my library (which I keep for various good reasons). So it is important to ask whether inspiration is simply divine providence, or whether it carries God's endorsement. Is God, in any sense, the *author* of inspired books?

I was hoping that in his later book, *Simply Christian*, Wright would have responded to this sort of question. But I cannot find there any improved definition or understanding of biblical inspiration. Chapter 13 of that book is titled "The Book God Breathed," and a subsection of that chapter is "God's Inspired Word."[25] But in that subsection Wright denies the dictation theory, as we have seen, propounds his metaphor of Scripture as a sacramental presence of God, and reiterates his view of the *purposes* for which God gave Scripture to us. He does not address the question of whether divine inspiration confers truth upon the biblical text.

He does mention the question, only to express his irritation with it:

> Though I'm not unhappy with what people are trying to affirm when they use words like "infallible" (the idea that the Bible won't deceive us) and "inerrant" (the stronger idea, that the Bible can't get things wrong), I normally resist using those words myself. Ironically, in my experience, debates about words like these have often led people away from the Bible itself and into all kinds of theories which do no justice to scripture as a whole—its great story, its larger purposes, its sustained climax, its haunting sense

24. *LW*, 37.
25. *SC*, 180–84.

of an unfinished novel beckoning us to become, in our own right, characters in its closing episodes.[26]

Yes, I too have seen and read about people who became so preoccupied with infallibility and so on that they missed out on other important biblical themes. Wright would say "more important biblical themes," but I am not sure. The biblical writers say over and over again that God's Word is true and is the truth (that's all that "inerrancy" means[27]). That must have been important to them. If, as on my suggested model, Scripture was the Constitution of Israel, its highest authority, the very Word of God, then of course to deny its infallibility would have been a great insult to God.

In *The Last Word*, Wright asks,

> Which is the bottom line: "proving the Bible to be true" (often with the effect of saying, "so we can go on thinking what we've always thought"), or taking it so seriously that we allow it to tell us things we'd never heard before and didn't particularly want to hear?[28]

Again, he pits the issue of truth against the issue of practical seriousness about Scripture. But are these really opposed? Indeed, why should we take the Bible with such seriousness if we don't believe it to be true?

And of course if Wright may report his experience, I have an equal right to report mine, which is that many people who *reject* the infallibility, the inerrancy, and the truth of Scripture often end up taking Scripture with very little seriousness. I find it hard to believe that this rejection and this sort of practice are never linked. Perhaps my experience is different from Wright's. But seriously, I think that both those who affirm and those who deny

26. *SC*, 183.

27. See the account of infallibility and inerrancy in my *Doctrine of the Word of God*, 167–76.

28. *LW*, 95; cf. 91, where he challenges readers to allow the Bible to cut across their "cherished traditions."

biblical infallibility need to attend to their practical responses to
the Bible. I suspect Wright would agree with me on this point. But
then the practical issue does not answer the question of whether
the Bible is a true document, or the question of whether we should
be concerned about its truth.

The question is simple. Given that God inspired the Bible, what
effect did that inspiration have on the biblical text? Did it make
that text true, reliable, even infallible, or did it leave that text as a
fallible book? Wright certainly treats the Bible as a true document,
and, as we have seen, he even says he is "not unhappy with what
people are trying to affirm when they use words like 'infallible' . . .
and 'inerrant.'"[29] But he stifles discussion of these concepts by a
one-sided comment about what this discussion sometimes leads
people to do. I still await a meaningful comment from Wright on
this important question.

If Wright's failure to address this issue is the new feature in his
"new view of biblical authority," then I confess that I prefer to stay
with the old view. If he thinks that this kind of talk enables us to
"transcend the Bible wars," I do not believe he has succeeded. The
question of the truth of Scripture will not go away. Some believe it
is true; some do not. But if it is not legitimate to *contend* over this
issue, if it is not worth fighting for, then I do not know what is. For
if the Bible is not true, it makes no sense for us to insert ourselves
into the narrative, to view Scripture as a sacramental dwelling of
God, or anything else.

I realize that the difference between Wright and myself is from
one perspective very small. Wright has told us that in Scripture
God *speaks* to us in language. Wright is sympathetic to people who
speak of infallibility and inerrancy, and his only criticism of those
concepts is that they may distract us from what Wright thinks are
more important questions. Certainly there is room in the church
for people to disagree over what questions are most important.

29. SC, 183.

Wright is certainly an ally in the Bible wars, even though he thinks he has gotten beyond them. I agree with him far more than I disagree. I think part of our difference stems from our different ethnicities. Wright and other European Christians are often critical of the American tendency to magnify the question of biblical infallibility. But why should anyone make a big deal of ethnicity in the church of Jesus Christ?

But I do think we need to make a big deal of the truth of the text of Scripture, and that that text does not just *happen* to be true. It is true because God has inspired that text, even more, that God has *authored* that text, since it is his Word. That is what God's breathing is, his speech. It would be, perhaps, only a small step for our dear brother N. T. Wright to agree with me, to move from mere sympathy for biblical infallibility and inerrancy to affirmation of these. As of now, he does not seem to see the importance of that affirmation, and this essay of mine is simply a brotherly attempt to remind him of it, and to remind all of us who respect N. T. Wright as a teacher of Scripture.

## SCHOLARSHIP ESTABLISHES WHETHER THE BIBLE IS HISTORICAL

As our last topic, I would like to mention one important implication of the points I have been making. It has to do with Wright's own approach to historical Bible scholarship. Since Wright prefers not to speak in traditional terms of Scripture's infallibility and inerrancy, one asks how he does evaluate its statements, particularly in historical matters. I focus on history here because of its intrinsic importance, because Wright is a biblical historian more than anything else, and because biblical history is, after all, the narrative Wright considers so central in his theology of Scripture. He says that the historicity of Scripture is important to him: although he challenges biblical literalists to rethink their assurances, he says, this "does not mean that I am indifferent to the question of whether the events written about in the gospels actually took place. Far from it."[30]

I mentioned earlier that Wright is more conservative than many biblical scholars in his evaluation of biblical history. As we have seen, Wright opposes the rationalist approach of the Enlightenment,[31] which led to "the muddled debates of modern biblical scholarship."[32] He is himself vitally concerned with "the question of whether the events written about in the gospels actually took place."[33] And for the most part his judgments are that these events did take place. But why does he come to this evaluation?

The main reason he mentions is the evidence brought by biblical scholars, of whom he is, of course, a leading representative. In *Simply Christian* he summarizes his scholarly conclusions on the reliability of the four Gospels[34] and on the truth of Jesus' resurrection.[35] In *The Last Word* he says that the way to combat "modernist" views of Scripture influenced by Enlightenment rationalism is

> to go further into serious historical work than modernism (for its own reasons) was prepared to do. When we do this, we discover again and again that many of the problems or "contradictions" discovered by modernist critical study were the result of projecting alien worldviews onto the text.[36]

Today, he says, biblical scholars have better resources than the old modernists had: lexicons, ancient texts, archaeological and numismatic discoveries. So, Wright continues,

> We should gratefully use all these historical resources. When we do so . . . we will discover that quite a bit of the old "modernist"

30. *LW*, 95.
31. Ibid., 87–88.
32. Ibid., 89.
33. Ibid., 95; cf. 112–13.
34. *SC*, 95–99.
35. *LW*, 112–16.
36. *SC*, 95.

consensus is challenged on the grounds to which it originally appealed—namely, serious historical reconstruction.

Christianity should be ready to give an answer about what really happened within history and how, within the historian's own proper discipline, we can know that with the kind of "knowledge" appropriate to, and available within, historical research.[37]

Note also that he says,

Assessing [the Gospels'] historical worth can be done, if at all, only by the kind of painstaking historical work which I and others have attempted at some length.[38]

So it appears that the scholar is the final arbiter of historical truth. Of course, according to Wright, we should not carry on this work the way the old modernists did. We can do so much better than they.

But there's something wrong with this. Wright is saying that historical scholars came up with conclusions radically contrary to Scripture until, say, 1980, but now we can turn their ideas completely around with the resources we have today. But who is to say that a hundred years from now the modernists—or some new movement in the modernist tradition—might not gain the upper hand? History is a human science, and it constantly changes in its methods and conclusions. Is Wright really so sure that his own methods and conclusions will endure forever?

It is interesting that in this discussion Wright mentions that one of the problems with modernism was its tendency toward "projecting alien worldviews onto the text." Does Wright think that scholars, even conservative scholars, can entirely avoid doing this today? Is the answer to try to avoid the use of any worldview, or to read the text in the light of one true worldview? Clearly he disapproves of

37. Ibid., 95–96.
38. Ibid., 99.

the modernists' use of their worldview, but he says nothing about the role of worldview, or what I would call presuppositions, in the work of historical scholarship.

I doubt myself whether anyone can read Scripture, or any other book, without any presuppositions at all. (That's the one statement about which I agree with Rudolf Bultmann.) And, to make a long story short, it seems obvious to me that Christian scholars should do their work out of a Christian worldview. So it is not just a matter of scholarship, and it is not just a matter of going and looking at the facts. It is a matter of looking at the facts in the right way.

How do we find the right way to look at facts? In my judgment, that is another function of Scripture. If Scripture is our highest authority, it must determine our fundamental presuppositions, our worldview.

I think Wright does this for the most part, though he never articulates it. It is not as though the modernists imposed an alien worldview on the text and Wright reads the text with no worldview at all. It is rather that Wright reads the Scripture assuming that God exists, that miracles like the resurrection of Christ are possible, that we live as part of the narrative of redemptive history. The Enlightenment rationalists assumed that miracles are not possible; Wright assumes that they are. If the rationalist consensus is a presupposition, then so is Wright's assumption. Wright ought to be up front about this.

And if he were to be explicit about his presuppositions, he would have to admit that we Christians believe, say, in the resurrection, not just because a new generation of historical scholars say we may, but also because the Bible says the resurrection occurred. What is missing in Wright as a historian is his willingness to say, even though I think he believes it, that the biblical history is true because the Bible says it is.

It is significant that in 1 Corinthians 15, Paul argues the reality of the resurrection, not only on the basis of historical witnesses and evidences (though he does do that), but also and primarily on the basis that the resurrection of Jesus was part of the apostolic preaching (1 Cor. 15:1–3, 11–12, 14). The Corinthians should believe in the resurrection, Paul says, not only because of historical evidence, but also—and primarily—because it is taught by the Word of God, by inspired apostles. For us, the equivalent point is that we should believe the resurrection because the Bible tells us to, because the Bible itself contains sufficient evidence, and because the evidence should be seen on biblical presuppositions.

If Wright understood that the Bible must control our thoughts to the deepest level, to our most fundamental presuppositions, he would not be so indifferent to questions about infallibility and inerrancy, which in the end are simply questions about the truth of Scripture. For if we embrace Scripture as our presupposition, we embrace it as our most fundamental criterion of truth. And our fundamental criterion of truth must itself be true. If Wright understood this, he would see that it is not scholarship alone that establishes the truth of Scripture, but scholarship through the lens of Scripture. Ultimately, what establishes the truth of Scripture is Scripture itself, and therefore scholarship that embraces the truth of Scripture.[39]

And that truth does not fade from age to age. "The grass withers, the flower fades, but the word of our God shall stand forever" (Isa. 40:8). Whatever new methods and ideas emerge among historical scholars, the Word of God remains. The church's fundamental understanding of Scripture has not changed since the time of the apostles—not because the standards of historical scholarship have remained constant over that time, for they have not; but because the church has always had the Word of God itself to stand as judge over its thinking. May God's Word continue, as he has promised, to guide us in our understanding of its truth.

39. In one sense that implies that it is Scripture that validates Scripture. I have discussed this kind of circularity in many places. See, for example, John M. Frame, *The Doctrine of the Knowledge of God* (Phillipsburg, NJ: Presbyterian and Reformed, 1985), 130–33. The fact is that any attempt to validate a final standard of truth and falsity must be circular in a sense, because it must appeal to its own standard, not some other.

# 7

# Did God Really Say?

## DAVID B. GARNER

IN HIS SERIES OF ESSAYS entitled *Is There A Text in This Class?*,[1] literary theorist Stanley Fish contends that meaning is a reader's construction. According to Fish, meaning resides neither in the text itself nor in original authorial intention. Meaning is a construction of the reader, or more precisely, the reader in a given cultural context.[2] This reader is no king of his own interpretive island; instead he operates in a culturally conditioned community, a communal context that fully governs his interpretation. It is this limiting communal factor that reels Fish in from absolute individu-

1. Stanley Fish, *Is There a Text in This Class? The Authority of Interpretive Communities* (Cambridge, MA: Harvard University Press, 1980).
2. Fish contends "that standards of right and wrong do not exist apart from assumptions, but follow from them" (ibid., 174). Kevin J. Vanhoozer, *Is There a Meaning in This Text? The Bible, the Reader, and the Morality of Literary Knowledge* (Grand Rapids: Zondervan, 1998), 57, rightly discerns the "neo-pragmatism" and self-centeredness of such a paradigm. "Truth—in metaphysics, morals, or meaning—is what we assign beliefs that seem good to us, beliefs that perform some useful purpose."

alism, as he attempts a *via media* between modernist rationalism (the text possesses objective meaning) and postmodern irrationalism (the text means whatever *I* want it to mean).

Fish thereby self-consciously distinguishes himself from the pure relativism of other postmodern philosophers, philologists, and literary critics. Yet Fish's method simply avoids drowning in postmodern individualistic relativism by plunging into a cultural version of the same.[3] Because the text has no meaning until the reader in community produces it, authorial intent and objective meaning get crushed beneath the wave of multiple-reader autonomy. Put another way, in the Fish school, meaning comes not *from* the words, but *to* the words. "In a real sense, for Fish, the commentary (viz., the work of interpretation) *precedes* the text."[4] Deconstructing the vitals of meaningful communication, Fish and other theorists have entirely reversed the stream of interpretation, forcing meaning upon texts rather than discerning meaning from them. This paradigm for reading represents a categorical shift, recentering meaning upon the interpreter and his method, and eclipsing the notion that interpretive method relies upon meaning resident in the text itself. Evidenced by the now virtually inexhaustible options for reader-based biblical interpretation, the Holy Scriptures themselves enjoy no immunity to these recalibrated, man-centered methods.

## CLARITY AND INTERPRETATION

### The Lords of Interpretation(s)

To be sure, few in evangelical scholarship have embraced this categorical shift in the *whole*; but even fewer have remained wholly uninfluenced by this revolutionized hermeneutical enterprise. While many still profess Scripture's authority, Scripture as divine Word has *functionally* handed its authoritative scepter to its readers

---

3. Vanhoozer, *Is There a Meaning in This Text?*, 169.
4. Ibid., 56.

and their thousands of interpretive schemes. This is not to say that all interpretive models now flatly ignore authorial intent, divine or human, but that the hermeneutical task has recentered upon the interpreter. Biblical and theological studies have a clearly appointed lord: it is you, the reader. Appropriately, Richard Gaffin dubs this the age of hermeneutics:

> Ours, it is fair to say, is a "hyperhermeneutical" age. Most readers do not need to be reminded how in recent decades issues of interpretation have burgeoned in an overwhelming, almost unbelievable fashion and taken on unprecedented dimensions. Projects for construing texts have become paradigms for constructing, or deconstructing, reality as a whole. But the net result of this intensive expenditure of hermeneutical energy is a crisis in hermeneutics, an increasing hermeneutical despair.[5]

As layers of hermeneutical methods continue to pile up, and the fossilized versions of prior generations lie beneath the scholarly silt, attaining a finally satisfying method would seem now hopeless. However, the perpetually inadequate paradigms that generate this "hermeneutical despair" have not dissuaded some from clinging to the hope of a final, clear hermeneutical victory. Following the well-worn groove, new reader-based interpretive methods appear unceasingly.

## Certainty and Uncertainty

This expanding number of interpretive methods elicits a strange blend of certainty and uncertainty. On the one hand, despite the vastly disparate and even impossible proposals for interpretation,[6]

5. Richard B. Gaffin, "Speech and the Image of God: Biblical Reflections on Language and Its Uses," in *The Pattern of Sound Doctrine: Systematic Theology at the Westminster Seminaries: Essays in Honor of Robert B. Strimple*, ed. David Van Drunen (Phillipsburg, NJ: P&R Publishing, 2004), 191.
6. A prime example of impossible interpretive complexity is that of William J. Webb in *Slaves, Women, and Homosexuals: Exploring the Hermeneutics of Cultural Analysis* (Downers Grove, IL: IVP Academic, 2001). Critiquing Webb's eighteen-step

the so-called advance of biblical scholarship in recent decades has produced a drunken narcissism. Uncertainty of methods and results persist, yet there abides an incongruous certainty about the right to autonomous method alongside a clarion call for the novice to trust in the scholars who really know what they are doing. At the center of this certainty/uncertainty imbroglio is the matter of biblical clarity.

As biblical studies (Ancient Near Eastern and Second Temple Judaistic) have advanced significantly, corresponding convictions about biblical clarity have inversely diminished. "Two hundred years ago, Bible readers only thought that they understood many passages that now we have doubts about. Paradoxically, our *subjective* sense of the clarity of Scripture seems diminished at the same time that we have *greater objective evidence* regarding the clear meaning of the Bible."[7] Discerning the hermeneutical temptations, Moisés Silva renders an admonition, employing Martin Luther's categories of clarity: we must not confuse the *external* and *internal* perspicuity of Scripture, and "we dare not attribute to Scripture the limitations of our hearts and minds."[8] His warning has gone largely unheeded. Even though biblical scholars may not draw anything other than provisional conclusions by their interpretive methods, many nonetheless exercise their methods on the assumption that clarity of understanding could still come *by reliance upon scholarly method.* Even if they have abandoned full perspicuity as a goal,[9] they cling relentlessly to their interpretive wares and even more feverishly to their right to cling to them.

---

hermeneutical method, Wayne Grudem asks incredulously about applying even the first methodological step, "*Who* will be able to do this?" Wayne Grudem, "'A Redemptive-Movement Hermeneutic: The Slavery Analogy' (Ch 22) and 'Gender Equality and Homosexuality' (Ch 23) by William J. Webb," *JBMW* 10, 1 (Spring 2005): 111 (emphasis added).

7. Moisés Silva, *Has the Church Misread the Bible? The History of Interpretation in the Light of Current Issues,* Foundations of Contemporary Interpretation (Grand Rapids: Zondervan, 1996), 70–71.

8. Ibid., 71.

9. As we will see below, casting perspicuity as a product of hermeneutics corrupts both perspicuity and hermeneutics.

A prime example of such self-confidence in scholarly competence is Kenton Sparks.[10] According to him, only a distinct class of gifted scholars is capable even to engage with biblical-historical criticism. Sparks contends that "as disciplines go, [Assyriology] is a very challenging field of study, which can only be mastered by men and women with unusual intellectual gifts and with a healthy work ethic."[11] He then concludes,

> First, and above all, historical-critical judgments are products of academic *expertise*, in which *intellectually gifted scholars* apply their respective trades to *very complex* linguistic and archaeological data from the ancient world. This means, of course, that in most cases *the average person is in no position to evaluate, let alone criticize*, the results of critical scholarship. Such a dictum applies not only to Assyriology but also to *every academic discipline*, both of the sciences and the humanities. Consequently, a *certain humility* is warranted when those *outside a scholarly discipline* wish to inquire about and evaluate the *tried and tested conclusions of scholars in that discipline.*[12]

While the text of Scripture fails Spark's clarity test, what is clear is his confidence in his own scholarly field. The call to humility evidently applies only to "those outside a scholarly discipline." If implicit kudos were not enough, Sparks presents himself as one of the academic elite deserving implicit trust: "I have already done my own weighing of the evidence and have concluded that in many instances, the critical consensus on the Bible is essentially correct and reasonably justified."[13]

10. Kenton L. Sparks, *God's Word in Human Words: An Evangelical Appropriation of Critical Biblical Scholarship* (Grand Rapids: Baker, 2008). The subtitle boldly proclaims his syncretizing agenda, in which he seeks to apply "believing criticism," a method that claims the Bible is error-ridden and yet remains God's Word.
11. Ibid., 58. He continues, "One purpose of this survey [of Assyriology] is to illustrate the sheer complexity of the ancient data and the extent of expertise needed to interpret it."
12. Ibid., 70 (emphasis added).
13. Ibid., 76.

In essence, we are called to put down our Bibles and pick up Sparks. The "average person" can learn what he needs to know solely from Sparks and his academic guild. Already in 1979, J. I. Packer complained of a "new papalism—the infallibility of the scholars."[14] Now three decades later, this scholarly guild, failing to be humbled by the shifting paradigms of its convictions, with blind (and desperate) self-adulation continues to speak, as it were, *ex cathedra*. Understanding will come to the lay reader only by reliance upon the amorphous Protestant academic Magisterium. Stanley Hauerwas sets the stakes in no uncertain terms: "Most North American Christians assume they have a right, if not an obligation, to read the Bible. I challenge the assumption. No task is more important than for the church to take the Bible out of the hands of individual Christians in North America."[15]

These condescending calls for trust in the scholarly guild are met, on the other hand, by a nagging uncertainty. Sparks himself wishes to maintain an air of humility in his conclusions, even when he calls for the implicit trust of the ill-equipped Bible student. Academia requires formal hermeneutical "humility." *Trust in me*, it is contended. *I may not know what I'm doing, but I certainly know more than you.* For those who cling to the slippery Fish hermeneutic, or even for those who believe that the chronological and cultural distance between the contemporary reader and the original text makes firm conclusions about original meaning impossible, any expression of conviction evidences modernist arrogance at best and scholarly foolishness at worst. Uncertainty is the only certainty;

14. J. I. Packer, *God Has Spoken: Revelation and the Bible* (Downers Grove, IL: InterVarsity Press, 1979), 21. Packer rightly notes that the church is actually indebted to the scholarly community for its aid in biblical understanding and exposition. Yet the "pathetic" paradox persists: the critical movement "has given the Church the Bible in a way that has deprived the Church of the Bible, and led to a famine of hearing the words of the Lord" (22).

15. Stanley Hauerwas, *Unleashing the Scriptures: Freeing the Bible from Captivity to America* (Nashville: Abingdon Press, 1993), 15.

provisionality or "epistemological modesty"[16] has become the only academically respectable position. This hermeneutic of uncertainty is praised as honest and humble, and the provisional ethos is lauded as a moral victory against the objective claims of modernism and the naïve assertions of fundamentalism.

Further, the hermeneutic of uncertainty serves to tone down the historically exclusive claims of Christianity, and to present a version that is gentler and less sectarian. Scripture certainly is not clear, it is argued. What remains clear, however, is the right of the hermeneutical expert both to postulate his theory and to expect others' respect in doing so. Moreover, the effective denial of biblical perspicuity is paraded as, or better contorted into, evidence of proper biblical humility. How, in the face of the Bible's own claims to clarity, an assertion of its lack of clarity can be considered humble is astounding. This artificial humility masks academic arrogance, supplanting the authoritative clarity of Scripture with hermeneutical craft. When I say that something is not clear that God has spoken clearly, I am hardly manifesting the doxological posture incumbent upon a student of Scripture. Denial of perspicuity is not humility; it is arrogance of the highest order.

### Clear Implications of an Unclear Word

Such arrogant commitments to biblical *im*perspicuity vitiate Christian vitality. Postmodern rejection of a clear Bible leaves no foundations on which to build except the immovable foundation that there are no foundations. Students enter many seminaries with questions about the Bible, and learning there that the Bible is a mess and that there are no definite answers, they graduate in unbelief. Standing before congregations who desperately long

16. Peter Berger, "Epistemological Modesty: An Interview with Peter Berger," *Christian Century*, October 29, 1997, 972–78, accessed September 10, 2011, http://www.religion-online.org/showarticle.asp?title=240; cf. David Brooks, "The Big Test," *New York Times*, February 23, 2009, accessed September 10, 2011, http://www.nytimes.com/2009/02/24/opinion/24brooks.html?_r=1.

for cogent answers to the cries of their souls, these new preachers find themselves able to deliver only hopelessly irrelevant rhetoric. Their hermeneutically ravaged minds promulgate anemia and sentimentality as they doggedly hold forth messages of milk toast and muffins. They have nothing definite to preach except the message that there is nothing definite to preach.

Most, concerned about their congregations, limp along caringly with warming stories, political analysis, sentimental journeys, moral philosophizing, and other ostensibly erudite pontification. Others still formally preach from their Bibles, but their preaching lacks the authoritative unction of biblical proclamation. When the preacher himself doubts the very message he preaches, he is in no place to declare, *Thus says the Lord*. Words flow from the tongue, but there is surely no sure Word, transcendently no transcendent message. Such lack of material conviction produces an impotent and irrelevant church more quickly than anything else.

In Western Christian communities of faith blessed with personal copies of Scripture, paltry interpretive paradigms manifest themselves not only in pulpits, but also in lay Bible study pursuits. Suffering under the deconstruction of meaning as a human and pragmatic creation, today's Bible reader often unwittingly conflates meaning and application. The most prominent question, it seems, is, "What does this verse mean *to me*?" Authority for interpretation begins with me in my situation and my own assessment of that situation. Coming to the Bible with an entrenched sense of entitlement, I engage the text, may even interest myself to some degree in its grammatical-historical context, and employ whatever skills I have at my disposal to derive a meaning from the text. But driving my interpretation is the prevailing *relevance* question—a relevance bordered and shaped by the parameters of my own knowledge and experience.

Though such a method lacks scholarly sophistication, it operates with some of the same assumptions: the text is there for me to massage for my own purposes. Whatever the interpretive conclusion, whether or not it is connected to the text and its context is not the final court of appeal. I am lord of the interpretive process. Meaning grounded in the text and authorial intention is traded for pragmatism; if it works in my own mind or for my current situation, the interpretation then is acceptable and is right for me. Unwittingly such a method adopts the Fish paradigm, and reduces perspicuity into a culturally conditioned, existentially pragmatic construction: It seems clear enough to me; therefore it is sufficiently clear.

Problems with this approach to Scripture are multifold. Lost is the certainty that God *can* and *has* spoken understandably. Lost is the functional authority of Scripture for interpretation, for belief, for practice. If real meaning derives from the reader, no redeeming clarity in biblical language exists in any meaningful sense. Scriptural authority shrivels and dies, because, "everything is a matter of interpretation, including interpretations described as core orthodoxy. We never have the crisp, unadorned voice of God."[17] *Jesus (I think) loves me (I think), this (I think) I know, for my community tells me so.* Clarity then is not a matter of text but of interpretive consensus, a consensus produced by the scholarly community or my community of faith. And despite the assertions of Fish, sometimes it is a consensus of one—the lone ranger, the would-be autonomous interpreter.

## Taking Aim at Perspicuity

Confronting the amorphous evangelical identity produced from Fish-friendly interpretive schemes, Christian Smith finds biblical perspicuity untenable. He critiques the "pervasive interpretive pluralism,"[18] the vast number of incompatible interpretations of

17. James K. A. Smith, *The Fall of Interpretation: Philosophical Foundations for a Creational Hermeneutic* (Downers Grove, IL: InterVarsity Press, 2000), 44, recorded in Mark D. Thompson, *Clear and Present Word: The Clarity of Scripture*, New Testament Studies in Biblical Theology 21 (Downers Grove, IL: InterVarsity Press, 2006), 35n56.

18. Christian Smith, *The Bible Made Impossible: Why Biblicism Is Not a Truly Evangelical Reading of Scripture* (Grand Rapids: Brazos Press, 2011), Kindle edition. This phrase occurs repeatedly throughout the book.

Scripture that defy any intrinsic clarity in the biblical text. Addressing "biblicists" who affirm supreme scriptural authority and perspicuity, yet assert incompatible theological interpretations, Smith contends that disparate interpretations and biblical perspicuity are irreconcilable. If the Bible were clear, Smith insists, then interpretations would not suffer their diverse and even mutually exclusive conclusions. "The good news of the evangelical Mennonite is very, very different from the good news of the conservative Republican evangelical."[19]

Smith spills ink on a number of theological themes (predestination, atonement, and gifts of the Holy Spirit, to name a few), about which he describes the polarized and polarizing positions. He claims that the divergence of views on these themes can be read only in a way that concludes that the Bible is inconclusive. So convinced is he of intramural theological incongruity that he asserts, "many scholars of American evangelicalism find it difficult to identify anything much that evangelicals share in common."[20] Smith's thesis of pervasive interpretive pluralism is grounded in his judgment of a pervasive biblical *imperspicuity*. To build his case, Smith accumulates a large mass of evidence that would seem to support the pervasive interpretive pluralism thesis. On the surface, his thesis may seem compelling. With unrestrained hermeneutical freedom, nothing is clear because no one agrees on anything theological. As rehearsed frequently by a former professor of mine: "Many things in the Bible I read, things that are put there by you and by me."

Smith's thesis is desperately flawed, however. In many cases, lack of interpretive agreement grows from a failure to give Scripture the final authority in matters of interpretation. Cultural, epistemological, and moral compromise distort our understanding. In his classic perspicuity debate with Erasmus, Luther writes, "I know that to many people a great deal remains obscure; but that is due, not to any lack of clarity in Scripture, but to their own blindness and dullness, in that they make no effort to see the truth which, in itself, could not be

19. Ibid., Kindle locations 807–8.
20. Ibid., Kindle location 882.

plainer."[21] But as Luther himself concedes, not all disagreement lies in lackluster laziness. Certain portions of Scripture are clearer than others, but Luther contends, the intended *meaning* of Scripture as a whole is transparent: "If words are obscure in one place, they are clear in another. What God has so plainly declared to the world is in some parts of Scripture stated in plain words, while in other parts it still lies hidden under obscure words. But when something stands in broad daylight also, it does not matter whether there is any evidence for it in the dark."[22] Luther highlights the fact that there is sufficient biblical clarity for shared evangelical belief. Yet Smith dismisses out of hand the idea that despite certain issues of hot debate, those who take the Bible seriously as the Word of God share core scriptural truth. In fact, it is from these core areas of agreement and the core commitment to the truthfulness of the Scriptures that meaningful disagreement stems.

Let us join Smith in getting more specific. The Bible teaches God's sovereignty and man's responsibility, and "biblicist" Calvinists and Arminians share those clearly revealed truths. It is clear biblically that *God* reigns, rules, and holds all things together. It is clear that *God* is the Creator and the Redeemer. It is also clear biblically that man is *responsible* to respond to the Almighty God for his salvation. Again Calvinists and Arminians agree. The theological parting of ways comes in the interpretive decisions employed in fuller integration of the biblical texts, how to weigh properly certain Scripture texts and theological points over others, and how to execute our cognitive conclusions with epistemological integrity. Consistent Calvinists leave perceived mystery in the hands of God and underscore the divine sovereignty texts as formative for the interpretation of the responsibility texts; consistent Arminians, by wishing to uphold human freedom and responsibility, answer the mystery by elevating the responsibility texts and granting mankind

21. Martin Luther, *The Bondage of the Will: A New Translation of* De Servo Arbitrio *(1525), Martin Luther's Reply to Erasmus of Rotterdam*, trans. J. I. Packer and O. R. Johnston (Westwood, NJ: Fleming H. Revell, 1957), 72.
22. Ibid., 71–72.

determinative function in relationship to God's sovereignty. The differences then between "biblicist" Calvinists and Arminians are, from one perspective, secondary.[23] Though some second-tier determinations create theological and ecclesiastical incompatibility, the contrasting interpretations occur in view of certain core agreements.

The interface between hermeneutics and Scripture's clarity has produced kerfuffles since early in the Reformation. In *The Bondage of the Will*, Martin Luther challenges Erasmus about the clarity of the Bible:

> Any who cannot see the aforementioned clarity, and blindly stumble in the sunlight of Scripture, thereby reveal, if they are godless, how mighty is the dominion and power of Satan over the sons of men, which prevents them hearing and grasping the plainest words of God, and makes them like men whom an illusionist has mesmerised into thinking that the sun is a cold cinder, or believing that a stone is gold. If they are godly, however, they are to be numbered among those of the elect who are led into a degree of error, in order that the power of God, without which we cannot see or do anything at all, may be displayed in us. For man's failure to grasp God's words does not spring from weakness of understanding, as you would suggest; indeed, there is nothing better for grasping God's words than weakness of understanding, for it was for the weak and to the weak that Christ came, and to them He sends His Word. No, the cause is the wickedness of Satan, who is enthroned and reigns over us in our weakness, and who himself resists the Word of God. If Satan did not do so, the whole world could be converted by a single word of God, heard once; there would be no need of more.[24]

23. This assertion about the secondary differences between Arminian and Reformed understanding of Scripture is decidedly *not* an attempt to belittle or to obscure these differences in interpretation. The differences *are* significant and they *do* matter. The specific point here is to highlight that these differences occur *because of certain vital theological agreements*, agreements that Smith belittles. By contrast, Christians and Muslims, for example, have no common theological ground.

24. Luther, *Bondage of the Will*, 133–34.

In no uncertain terms, Luther exposes the spiritual source of interpretive chaos. The problem is not Scripture, but its readers.

An array of biblical interpretations on multiple biblical themes ought not then lead us to Smith's hopeless conclusions. Despite his amassed evidence, Smith grants inadequate credence to certain crystal-clear truths expressed in Scripture and the resulting understanding shared by many. More to our point, Smith not only overstates his case, but erroneously levels his rifle scope upon Scripture itself instead of on the slippery hermeneutics of much evangelical scholarship. Eyeing the varying human—individual, ecclesial, or communal—interpretations, Smith determines that disparate conclusions derive from biblical imperspicuity rather than from faulty human hermeneutical methods, and he ruinously shoots down Scripture's inherent, self-interpreting, clarion authority.

The Erasmus/Luther debate largely centered on authority in interpretation, as Luther, in the face of Roman Catholic interpretive control, discerned the Bible's self-attesting and self-interpreting authority, calling the church to operate *under* that authority.[25] Luther pleads with his formidable opponent, who maintained the need for the magisterial teaching authority of the church, "May I ask you, my dear Erasmus, to bear with my want of eloquence, as I in these matters bear with your want of knowledge."[26] We plead similarly with Christian Smith, who in his denial of biblical perspicuity erects overstated arguments that do not withstand the core theological consensus of biblical Christianity. His misdiagnosis of the cause of pervasive interpretive pluralism drives him to a *non sequitur*—that multiple interpretations rebut perspicuity. Moreover, what he himself conveniently neglects is that the Roman Catholic Church evidences no track record of consistency on a host of biblical and theological issues. He trades alleged Protestant instability for the moving target

---

25. The church's role in the history of interpretation is most important. Where Rome goes awry is in its self-appointed function as an authority on par with Scripture rather than beneath it.
26. Luther, *Bondage of the Will*, 65.

of the Roman Magisterium.[27] Most destructively, he denies the neces-sary and clear claims of Scripture to its own perspicuity, a move that effectively pits the divine authority of Scripture against the derivative authority of the church *and* against his own critical analysis.

## Perspicuity and Community: James Callahan

James Callahan has sought to rescue biblical perspicuity by seeking an elucidating exchange between author, text, and reader. Rejecting a reader hermeneutic on the one hand, he explicitly resists the "self-evidentiary nature of Scripture's clarity."[28] In large measure, Callahan wisely rejects any simplistic importation of modern historiographical expectation upon the text of Scripture. He stiffens against the herme-neutical calisthenics employed by some in the "Battle for the Bible" movement of the 1970s and 1980s who sought to impose simplistic explanations for apparent inconsistencies between Scripture passages. He creatively profiles the rationale: "The premise, then, is that the reason we affirm Scripture's clarity is due to Scripture's obscurity."[29]

Introducing his approach, Callahan argues "for the threefold, mutually dependent, practice of Scripture's texture, its reading and its readers."[30] He blends Scripture's use in community, how Scripture is represented idiosyncratically in that Christian community, and Scripture's engagement with the Christian reader in the community; these three "converge in the subject of Scripture's clarity."[31] Callahan contends, "The expression *clarity of Scripture* refers to how Chris-tians account for the union of Scripture that is read, an appropriate reading of Scripture and Scripture's readers. Scripture, when read in a Christian manner, can be said to be clear in itself but not by itself

27. Smith writes about his journey to Roman Catholicism in *How to Go from a Good Evangelical to a Committed Catholic in Ninety-five Difficult Steps* (Eugene, OR: Wipf and Stock, 2011).

28. James Callahan, *The Clarity of Scripture: History, Theology, and Contemporary Literary Studies* (Downers Grove, IL: InterVarsity Press, 2001), 25.

29. Ibid., 29.

30. Ibid., 24.

31. Ibid., 14.

(it has never been isolated from its readings or readers, historically or theologically)."[32] In one very important way, Callahan is correct. A claim to Scripture's clarity becomes an abstraction apart from consideration of the hearer; both speaker and receptor must exist for communication actually to *function* perspicuously. But the proper integration of perspicuity and interpretation requires careful distinctions, and though integrally connected, perspicuity and hermeneutics are not interdependent. The failure to distinguish hermeneutics from the *nature* of Scripture creates a lethal confusion between object and subject, revelation and illumination, external and internal perspicuity (Luther), divine word and human reception of that word.

Callahan insists, "The clarity of the text's meaning is not simply 'in' the text apart from how the Scripture is treated but has to do with how we read Scripture as Christians."[33] In this way, Callahan relocates perspicuity away from the Bible, making scriptural clarity contingent upon the reader's understanding and turning perspicuity into an interpretive matter rather than an essential, textual matter. For him, perspicuity is not about the nature of Scripture; it is a function of community hermeneutics. Conflating the objective and the subjective, Callahan's framework falls right into the hands of Christian Smith's pervasive interpretive pluralism. With Fish-like affinities, Callahan's perspicuity has a new home, the community of readers, where "Scripture [is] read by Christians in a Christian manner."[34]

## CLARITY AND SCRIPTURE

### Perspicuity and Hermeneutics

As historically articulated, perspicuity is attributive; it describes what Scripture *is*. The divine words of Scripture are breathed out by God (2 Tim. 3:16), and they clearly and accessibly convey what God intends them to convey. Perspicuity presupposes divine sovereignty,

32. Ibid., 11.
33. Ibid., 50.
34. Ibid., 14.

divine simplicity, and purposeful and effectual condescension through human language. Accordingly, WCF 1.7 presents biblical perspicuity in terms of its lucid central redemptive core and its resultant accessibility to its readers:

> All things in Scripture are not alike plain in themselves, nor alike clear unto all: yet those things which are necessary to be known, believed, and observed for salvation, are so clearly propounded, and opened in some place of Scripture or other, that not only the learned, but the unlearned, in a due use of the ordinary means, may attain unto a sufficient understanding of them.

Using negation ("not" and "nor") to center perspicuity in the gospel message ("for salvation"), this section pithily upholds the distinction between, yet inseparability of, resident clarity ("alike plain in themselves") and reader understanding ("alike clear unto all"). Authoritative clarity and clear authority are properties of Scripture, not (hoped for) consequences of its reading. On the other hand, the voice of Scripture does not issue forth in a vacuum. Clarity only retains intelligibility in view of its clarity *to the hearer*, but Scripture's clarity *depends* upon neither reader nor community. To be sure, Scripture's clarity is wed to its covenant purpose: communication to the people of God. God's personal and perspicuous revelation always has in view its intended hearer, but the interpretation of that clear revelation must remain carefully distinguished from the revelation itself.

Distinguishing hermeneutics from the nature of Scripture, in fact, is essential to maintaining the integrity of both. To reiterate, clarity is not a hermeneutical creation, but a biblical characteristic; clarity is a property of Scripture not a product of its interpretation.[35] Stated otherwise, perspicuity is not a doctrine of the understanding of Scripture, but of the understandability of Scripture. Scripture is not understandable because it is understood; it is understood

---

35. "Clarity is a property *of Scripture*, not a property of its readers," Wayne Grudem, "The Perspicuity of Scripture," *Themelios* 34, 3 (2009): 295.

because it is understandable. Yet the interrelation of hermeneutics and perspicuity is vital because perspicuity *purposes* understanding in the reader, and in this sense cannot be separated from him. Biblical hermeneutics depends on biblical perspicuity, and thus while interpretive method is, when rightly configured, wholly dependent upon the perspicuous text of Scripture, hermeneutics do not produce perspicuity any more than hermeneutics produce scriptural authority. Thus, as Luther stated to Erasmus, lack of understanding the intended meaning of Scripture does not evidence a problem with the Speaker and his speech, but evidences the moral and epistemological resistance of the hearer (cf. Rom. 1:18–32; 1 Cor. 1–2).

Because of the clarity of Scripture, WCF 1.9 expressly acquiesces to Scripture's own final interpretive authority: "The infallible rule of interpretation of Scripture is the Scripture itself: and therefore, when there is a question about the true and full sense of any Scripture (which is not manifold, but one), it must be searched and known by other places that speak more clearly." The Bible speaks clearly and the interpreter *depends* upon its clarity. If one text is less clear than another, the clearer text serves to guide the interpreter in understanding the less clear text. The reader is receptor, not creator. According to the WCF, the perspicuous authority of the Scripture enables genuine interpretive method. Moreover, the other classically articulated attributes of Scripture—authority, necessity, and sufficiency—require scriptural clarity. Apart from its perspicuity, Scripture cannot claim any meaningful authoritative voice for its hearers, carry out any necessary redemptive function in the lives of its hearers, nor serve the demands of sufficiency for the obedience of its hearers. As the Protestant church has insisted for generations, Scripture *is* clear, intrinsically and authoritatively clear.[36] Because of whose Word it is, it can be nothing less.

36. The historic doctrine of perspicuity does not neglect the difficult texts of Scripture nor does it dismiss Scripture's own claims to interpretive challenge (cf. 2 Peter 3:14–16). See Thompson, *Clear and Present Word*, 102–10, for an adept treatment of Scripture's alleged opacity.

## Who Says?

God is history's first speaker. From the very first chapter of Genesis and throughout the entire canon of Scripture, God conveys his will and his purpose using words. He himself makes clear that his words are clear. But even before he condescends to speak with mankind, according to the first chapters of Genesis, God spoke the worlds into existence. Words in the mouth of the Creator bore sufficient power to create vital elements out of nothing: that which was not came into existence and that which was inanimate became animate. Such efficacy of speech staggers the finite mind. But there is more. In direct obedience to the authoritative Word, the elements of creation in Genesis 1 submit to the words of God by carrying out the role he commands. That which was without existence is *by divine fiat* given existence, function, and the divinely endowed energy to carry out that function.[37]

Divine words at man's special creation beckon even greater marvel. Granted a stunning glimpse into primeval discourse, we find the Creator speaking uniquely about his crowning creation: "Let us make man in our image, after our likeness" (Gen. 1:26–27). This privileged peering into the heavenly monologue unambiguously establishes that communication is no human creation, but is first the province of God. Genesis unashamedly presents a God who speaks and a God whose "capacity for speech is treated as self-evident and operates as one of the most basic and influential assumptions in Scripture. Even the tempter does not doubt that God has spoken, merely what God has said (Gen. 3:1)."[38] Creating all things from nothing, God's words possess unfettered efficacy. Embedded into his words is real and clear meaning, and as evidenced by the response of even the subhuman creation, this meaning was understood. The prelapsarian context is

37. John H. Walton, *The Lost World of Genesis One: Ancient Cosmology and the Origins Debate* (Downers Grove, IL: InterVarsity Press, 2009), has argued that Genesis 1 presents a functional ontology. While Walton provides some suggestive insights from the Ancient Near Eastern world, his argument fails to give sufficient consideration to the prominent *ex nihilo* contours of the creation account and to the instruction of Scripture elsewhere (e.g., Heb. 11:1–3).

38. Thompson, *Clear and Present Word*, 60.

one of implicit and explicit obedience to the words of God; everything from the dust to the days responds to the command of the Creator.

The nature of divine communication begs for further investigation, so let us dig briefly into intra-Trinitarian mystery. According to Calvin, God is an "utterly simple unity";[39] he is a "single, simple essence";[40] "the essence of the one God is simple and undivided" and this essence "belongs to the Father, the Son, and the Spirit".[41] Yet at the same time, "by a certain characteristic the Father differs from the Son, and the Son from the Spirit."[42] Divine simplicity[43] involves eternal and unencumbered intra-Trinitarian fellowship, and unambiguous triune communication. For simplicity to be simple, for perfect unity to exist within the Godhead, intra-Trinitarian communication must occur with unobstructed purity and seamless fluidity. Thus, divine intra-Trinitarian communication is internally and eternally perspicuous, for God is infinite in his self-understanding; the omni-competent Spirit knows "the thoughts of God" (1 Cor. 2:11b ).

We could easily get lost here in the complexities of the "cease-less movement of perichoresis,"[44] but let us not miss the central point about intra-Trinitarian relationship. God is fully coherent, ultimately and eternally consistent, and an integral component of his perfect unity is his divine communication. That God is "true" (John 3:33) then renders a verbal snapshot of the integrity, whole-ness, and simplicity of God. His communication necessarily reflects

39. John Calvin, *Institutes of the Christian Religion*, ed. John T. McNeill, trans. Ford Lewis Battles, 2 vols. (Philadelphia: Westminster, 1960), 1.13.19.

40. Ibid., 1.13.20.

41. Ibid., 1.13.22.

42. Ibid.

43. By "simplicity" we intend the historic meaning of this theological concept, wherein God is not a conglomeration of parts, but is One wholly unified Being. "Every attribute of God is identical with his essence," Herman Bavinck, *Reformed Dogmatics*, ed. John Bolt, trans. John Vriend, 4 vols. (Grand Rapids: Baker, 1992–2008), 2:173; cf. Heinrich Heppe, *Reformed Dogmatics*, trans. G. T. Thomson (London: George Allen and Unwin, Ltd., 1950), 112–23; Charles Hodge, *Systematic Theology*, 3 vols. (Peabody, MA: Hendrickson, 1999), 1:369–72.

44. Robert Letham, *The Holy Trinity: In Scripture, History, Theology, and Wor-ship* (Phillipsburg, NJ: P&R Publishing, 2004), 327.

this eternally harmonious personality, and as a manifestation of the noncomposite and absolute perfection of his being, God's eternal intra-Trinitarian communication suffers no ambiguity, misunderstanding, or interpretive fallacies. Speaking analogically, we can say that his intra-Trinitarian "speech"[45] is fluid, flawless, and self-attesting; it is perfectly spoken, perfectly understandable, and perfectly understood. Expressed in popular speech-act theory verbiage, in the divine locution, divine illocution and divine perlocution are eternally coterminous. In the Godhead exist no unintended perlocutions.[46]

Divine, intra-Trinitarian communication is eternally and necessarily clear; it is exhaustively perspicuous because God is God.

## Speech and the Imago Dei

But what of God's communication to man? It is surely one thing to insist on the intra-Trinitarian communion as pure, perfect, and without compromise. It surely is another to insist upon the perspicuity of divine speech to finite mankind. Does not man's createdness present an unbridgeable chasm for delivering and receiving comprehensible words of God? Do not God's transcendence and the integrity of the Creator/creature distinction prohibit a communicative point of contact for God with man? By the condescending kindness of this Triune God, we find actually the opposite.

As just seen, the Creator's communication is no tertiary component of the contours of the Bible's opening chapters. Rather, from the very beginning, the communication and self-revelation of God take center stage. His accommodating speech is intentional, substantial, and personal, and as such renders personal

45. "Speech" is best understood as accommodated divine communication in creation, and only by analogy coincides with the personal, nontemporal communication within eternal, intra-Trinitarian fellowship.

46. For an explanation of locution, illocution, and perlocution, see, for example, Jeannine K. Brown, *Scripture as Communication: Introducing Biblical Hermeneutics* (Grand Rapids: Baker, 2007), 32–35.

accountability to his hearers. His Word claims clarity, power, and efficacy. From the beginning we are presented with the uniquely superior and efficacious words of God: "And God said, 'Let there be light,' and there was light" (Gen. 1:3). But God speaks not only his creation into being; he speaks *to* the creation he has made. In condescending kindness, God engages his creation. In fact, he speaks directly to his creation, with his creating speech climaxing in the covenant he makes with those created *in his image* (Gen. 2:16–17). This speech to his people continues throughout redemptive history. Thus from the very opening chapters of Genesis, the God of Scripture reveals himself as not just a speaking God, but a God who speaks to *his* people. Covenant relationship requires covenant communication.

For this reason, communication is not only a divine characteristic, but also a divine entrustment. Mankind, created in God's image, communicates because God communicates. "We must be insistent that human language is not ultimately a human invention, but God's gift, a gift reflective of his own capacities as the Giver."[47] Thus language finds its origins not in cultural anthropology or evolutionary progress, but in God himself, whose communication is a matter of necessary habit: "The persons of the Trinity function as members of a language community among themselves."[48] As God's image-bearers, "we are made like [God], and that is why we can speak."[49] Beyond that, we are made like God and designed to understand his clear speech. We listen and understand because God, the first Speaker, has made us receptors of his speech, a privilege that simply cannot be overstated. Neither can we overstate the obligation to obey. Because language originates with the triune God,[50] language effectively conveys meaning and does so with clarity, as such clarity is a necessary characteristic of

47. Gaffin, "Speech and the Image of God," 191.
48. Vern S. Poythress, *In the Beginning Was the Word: Language—A God-Centered Approach* (Wheaton, IL: Crossway, 2009), 18.
49. Ibid., 9.
50. Ibid., 28.

divinely bestowed linguistic capacity.[51] Coherence and intelligibility characterize human language at the most foundational level, not because of any autonomous cognitive capacities of man, but because he is made as a communicative being in the image of his communicative Creator.

While the fall, of course, has corrupted our communication, the point here is that human communication is a pure gift for relationship, which is in its origin necessarily perspicuous. So, Richard Gaffin rightly concludes, "Our language is not innately ambiguous."[52] Just as we speak of nearsightedness in relation to sight and do not comprehend sight as the lack of myopia, so coherence in language is the norm from which the aberration is defined. Misunderstanding in language occurs in the context of essential understanding. Incoherence is flawed coherence; coherence is not flawed incoherence. Miscommunication is flawed communication; communication is not flawed miscommunication.

God's communicative intention with regard to man will not be frustrated (Isa. 55:10–11). Just as he created the sun and positioned it to give light to the earth, so God created man to receive the beams of his self-revelation. Having made man in his image and for a divinely determined purpose, God will not let that purpose fail. "The ultimate guarantee that God's word will be heard and understood, that it will achieve the purpose for which it was spoken and written, is the power and goodness of God himself."[53] To expand a bit, in his power and goodness God made man and woman in his image, with the full capacity to hear, understand, and speak. Hence, the authority of God's speech does not lose its integrity when he speaks to man. Having designed them as fully adequate receptors of his accommodating revelation, God explicitly called Adam and Eve to listen to his Word. Divine will is conveyed

51. Cf. ibid., 29–33.
52. Gaffin, "Speech and the Image of God," 191.
53. Thompson, *Clear and Present Word*, 111.

clearly in the selected words, and the almighty God has chosen to preserve these words in Holy Scripture.[54]

John Frame argues, "Divine authorship is the ultimate reason why Scripture is authoritative."[55] Indeed. And what we must also not overlook is how divine authorship is the ultimate reason why Scripture is *clear*. Perspicuity of divine words necessarily exists because of the Speaker's identity, the eternally coherent God, who has condescended to communicate clearly to those made in his image. In his accommodated speech, the Creator God does not stammer, and made like unto God we are designed to receive his communication in a coherent, meaningful manner. "Human beings are images of God and akin to God and by means of religion stand in a direct relation to God. The nature of this relation implies that God can both objectively and subjectively reveal himself to human beings created in his image."[56] And indeed God did reveal himself to man plainly, fully grounding man's responsibility. Rather than viewing the Creator/creature distinction as an obstacle to understanding, we must rather see that our very creation in God's image establishes clear duty to God's Word, an ontological imperative, a religious obligation to obey the covenantal demands expressed in the perspicuous words of our Creator.

God's Word is clear to us because he made us in his image.

## Perspicuity and Illumination

Some may protest that just because God's speech to Adam was clear does not mean that the revelation of God is clear to *fallen* humanity. How can we maintain a doctrine of perspicuity in a post-fall context? To be sure, the noetic effects of sin are hardly negligible. Sin's corruption thoroughly warps human understanding,

---

54. Grudem provides a summary of the explicit claims of the Old and New Testaments to its own clarity in "The Perspicuity of Scripture," 291–93.

55. John M. Frame, *The Doctrine of the Word of God* (Phillipsburg, NJ: P&R Publishing, 2010), 165.

56. Bavinck, *Reformed Dogmatics*, 1:308.

and in fact, the unending range of human interpretive schemes parades human intellectual distortion and insufficiency. But to make the inability to interpret divine speech correctly a rebuttal against perspicuity evidences ruinous category confusion. That corrupted man misunderstands and misrepresents God does not indicate a problem with the Revealer. Such a contention is a case of culpable transference, wherein we blame our misunderstanding on the Speaker rather than upon our own corruption. Surely human corruption from the fall does not corrupt divine speech! The problem is not with the clear speech, but with the rebellious creature, who cries out in unbelief, "*It is not I, Lord, but the words you have given me!*" Rather, it is the mind of man that needs changing for the Word of God, not the Word of God that needs changing for the mind of man.

Thus the redemptive gift of illumination is essential to understanding Scripture. Illumination coordinates with perspicuity because the Spirit of Truth illumines us to the resident and vital meaning of Scripture. We understand Scripture not because the Holy Spirit takes that which is opaque or translucent and makes it transparent; instead, we understand Scripture because the Holy Spirit transforms us, removing the moral blinders from our hearts' eyes and enabling us to see Scripture *for what it is* (cf. 2 Tim. 3:16–17; 2 Peter 1:19–21). Perspicuity provides the objective basis for illumination; illumination is not the basis for perspicuity. The perspicuous Scripture remains forever perspicuous, so that while illumination and perspicuity are inseparable, they remain necessarily distinct. Illumination does not change Scripture, it changes us.

### Perspicuity and Divine Will

According to Romans 1, the unspoken words of creation communicate clearly, even irresistibly. Creation is a tireless spokesman, perpetually affirming not only the existence of but also the character, or we might say, the God-ness, of God (Ps. 19). Its unrelenting voice bellows the sovereign, invisible attributes of the Creator, and with surround sound symphonic eloquence renders mankind wholly accountable to him. The persistent preacher pronounces the exclusivity of this one true God, not generic divinity or even generic theism. If the revelation were not sufficiently perspicuous, actual human accountability would be falsified. But instead, general revelation effectively communicates these personal truths according to the clear will of the Creator himself.

As a verbal form of revelation divulging God's redemptive grace, biblical content distinctively exposes love, mercy, and forgiveness. This special revelation does not resort to foreign tools of communication outside the sphere of creation, outside the larger context of revelation. "God is the primeval speaker, the originator not just of language in some vague and celestial sense, but of language addressed to and understood by human beings. It is his gift to us, a means of relationship that he is the first to use, not something alien that he commandeers or appropriates for this purpose."[57] In one sense, then, special revelation is properly seen as a subset of God's total revelatory activity; furthermore, the organic connection between natural and supernatural revelation exists because the one God reveals himself in both. Special revelation will then not speak *against* general revelation, but rather, as Cornelius Van Til insightfully puts forth, these forms of revelation presuppose and supplement one another.[58]

Both forms of revelation occur in the context of history, a history governed by the Author of it, who is revealing "a grand scheme of covenant revelation of himself to man."[59] Contemplating Paul's arguments in Romans 1, Van Til insists that the general revelation sufficiently accomplishes its purpose. The reason for its sufficiency is captured well by G. C. Berkouwer, who properly links the divine

57. Thompson, *Clear and Present Word*, 79.
58. Cornelius Van Til, "Nature and Scripture," in *The Infallible Word: A Symposium by the Members of the Faculty of Westminster Theological Seminary*, ed. N. B. Stonehouse and Paul Woolley, 2nd ed. (Philadelphia: Presbyterian and Reformed 1967), 267.
59. Ibid.

*intention* of revelation with its *sufficiency*: "it all depends *how* and *with what purpose* this revelation comes to man."[60] And thus, Berkouwer concludes, "Van Til surely was not wrong in emphatically asserting the *sufficiency* of general revelation."[61] God communicates his purpose effectively; what God intends to be clear, he reveals clearly.

In short, perspicuity exists qualitatively because of the divine will to reveal. Divine sovereignty and divine intention vouchsafe revelational perspicuity. Scripture, as inscripturated Word, authoritatively communicates in ways that surpass nonverbal revelation. Because special revelation is word revelation, it intensifies, codifies, and graciously expands the content delivered in general revelation. "It is God's desire to be known by his creatures, freely to enter into a relationship with them, to share with them the fellowship that is a feature of his own eternal nature, to invite them into his rest."[62] Employing words to achieve his divine redemptive ends, the Lord God succeeds in accomplishing what he intends.

## Perspicuity and Redemptive History

In his inaugural lecture to Princeton Theological Seminary in 1894, Geerhardus Vos affirmed, "The formation of the Scriptures serves no other purpose than to perpetuate and transmit the record of God's self-disclosure to the human race as a whole."[63] Scripture presents itself unmistakably as this gracious, self-disclosing revelation of almighty God. In his pithy encapsulation of redemptive history, the author of Hebrews introduces God as the Speaker. In ages past God has spoken through the prophets; in these last days, he has spoken with qualitatively superior speech in his Son

60. G. C. Berkouwer, *General Revelation* (Grand Rapids: Eerdmans, 1955), 312.
61. Ibid.
62. Thompson, *Clear and Present Word*, 51.
63. Geerhardus Vos, "The Idea of Biblical Theology as a Science and as a Theological Discipline," in *Redemptive History and Biblical Interpretation: The Shorter Writings of Geerhardus Vos*, ed. Richard B. Gaffin Jr. (Phillipsburg, NJ: Presbyterian and Reformed, 1980), 6.

(Heb. 1:1–2). Divine revelation is intentional and purposeful (Heb. 6:17), grounds our hope (Heb. 6:18–19), and renders the hearer fully accountable. The culminating exhortation, "See that you do not refuse him who is speaking" (Heb. 12:25a), resounds with the intensified eschatological force of the resurrected and exalted Son of God (cf. Heb. 2:1–4; 4:15; 5:10).[64]

God determined that he would reveal himself over the course of history by a mounting, telescopic disclosure. As the architectural metaphor of Hebrews 3:1–6 depicts, revelation comes progressively, successively, cumulatively.[65] Block upon block, the history of revelation works toward the completed revelatory edifice. "It isn't all given to us in Genesis chapter one. God built up the message, line upon line, precept upon precept, as the church was able to bear."[66] As part of the formative stages of the building project, God's speech in the Old Testament was incomplete; but even the reality of incompleteness was itself perspicuous. "The Old Testament believer's knowledge of God had a future orientation, one that generates a certain restlessness in the narrative and the prophetic material alike."[67] The author of Hebrews makes this point explicit; the saints of old knew that their stages in redemptive history were anticipatory (Heb. 11:8–16; cf. 1 Peter 1:10–12). They recognized Old Testament revelation as both perspicuously redemptive and restlessly sub-eschatological. Their "already" was entirely the "not yet."

The cumulative character of revelation, however, ought not draw us to conclude that God's revelation lacked clarity at any stage. Though prior to Christ's coming revelation remained incomplete, its intended meaning for the people of God at each particular point of history was sufficiently clear. Perspicuity then

---

64. See David Peterson, "God and Scripture in Hebrews," in *The Trustworthiness of God: Perspectives on the Nature of Scripture*, ed. Paul Helm and Carl Trueman (Grand Rapids: Eerdmans, 2002), 135–36.

65. Cf. Vos, "Idea of Biblical Theology," 12–13.

66. Donald Macleod, *A Faith to Live By: Understanding Christian Doctrine* (Fearn, Ross-shire, UK: Christian Focus, 1998), 29.

67. Thompson, *Clear and Present Word*, 57.

derives from divine competency and divinely appointed historical intention, not eschatological fulfillment. God's speech over the course of history does not become clearer, but the content of his speech becomes fuller, in Christ attaining its fullness. As Turretin insists, "God . . . cannot be said either to be unwilling or unable to speak plainly without impugning his perfect goodness and wisdom."[68] It pleased God to reveal himself over the course of history in successive stages, with the mounting crescendo reaching its finale in the Lord Jesus Christ. Thus, revelation is clear at each stage according to the wise purposes of God, and the eschatological revelation in Jesus Christ, the Son of God, completes these redemptive purposes. The fact that revelation concludes in Christ, however, does not suggest that Christ appears only in New Testament revelation.

Augustine, speaking of both Old and New Testaments, affirms, "I find Christ everywhere in those books."[69] The gospel of the Son of God is actually preached to Abraham (Gal. 3:8) and promised "through his prophets in the holy Scriptures" (Rom. 1:2). Thus, the assertion of Christ's presence in Old Testament revelation is not merely a function of a novel hermeneutic applied by Jesus Christ and his apostles. Christ explains his substantive presence in the Old Testament *because he is there*, not because he hijacks the Old Testament with inventive, reinterpretive schema (cf. Rom. 1:1–2; Heb. 1:1–2; 3:1–6). As the Son of God himself expresses, the failure to see *him* as the substance of the Old Testament is morally culpable. Such a blinded reading of Scripture exposes a sin problem, not an opaque text problem. Indeed Jesus' rebuke of the religious leaders of his day (John 5:39–47) and of his own disciples (Luke 24:25) possesses integrity only if the Old Testament Scriptures are in themselves perspicuously Christ-revealing.

68. Francis Turretin, *Institutes of Elenctic Theology*, ed. James T. Dennison, trans. George Musgrave Giger, 3 vols. (Phillipsburg, NJ: P&R Publishing, 1992), 1:145.

69. Augustine, *Contra Faustum*, A Select Library of the Nicene and Post-Nicene Fathers of the Christian Church 1 (Grand Rapids: Eerdmans, 1989), 4:192.

While it is true that "he interpreted to them in all the Scriptures the things concerning himself" (Luke 24:27b), this interpretation must not be viewed as eisegesis, but as an act faithful to the actual content of the Scriptures. In fact, Luke makes explicit that Jesus' post-resurrection explanations "opened their minds to understand the Scriptures" (Luke 24:45). Rather than introducing a manipulative hermeneutic and imposing it on the text of Scripture, Jesus illumines the text by opening the mind of his hearers. He takes the already clear Word and explains its clarity to a hearer who previously had not heard, to a seer who had not seen, to an interpreter who had not rightly interpreted. The fully disclosed Word incarnate explains the fully clear Word inscripturated, and does so by enabling his disciples to see in the Word of God what is already there.

Inasmuch as Scripture is centered on the redemptive work of Jesus Christ, perspicuity is tethered securely to history, a history of revelatory word and deed that is sovereignly directed by the God of heaven. Working on the stage of history Almighty God accomplishes his good purposes *at his appointed time.* Word revelation then interlocks with deed revelation in such a way that redemptive deeds are sufficiently and perspicuously interpreted for the people of God. So Geerhardus Vos contends, "As soon as we realize that revelation is at almost every point interwoven with and conditioned by the redeeming activity of God in its wider sense, and together with the latter connected with the natural development of the present world, its historic character becomes perfectly intelligible and ceases to cause surprise."[70] In other words, biblical revelation occurs according to divinely orchestrated purposes in the unfolding of human history, binding divine word and divine deed. Thus, revelation was no less perspicuous for the Israelites at Mount Sinai than it was for the church after Pentecost. The difference between these two scenes of revelation is epochal: one of forward-looking revelation in process and the other of revelation eschatologically completed. In both stages, however, the revelation, given with all wisdom and

70. Vos, "Idea of Biblical Theology," 8.

grace by God himself, was sufficiently clear to the people for their needs at their particular time in history. Summarily, the historically conditioned purposes of God in revelation provide the parameters for perspicuity, as God reveals clearly and purposefully what he wishes, when he wishes.

In this way the canon of Scripture necessarily comes to the fore. Just as God acted intentionally in redemptive deed revelation (e.g., the Exodus), he spoke intentionally in redemptive word revelation. His various interpretive words about his redemptive acts sufficiently elucidate his particular purposes in history. Precisely as the redemptive deeds of God function in overarching interconnectedness, so biblical perspicuity must not be treated atomistically. While God makes his redemptive purpose clear, this permeating teleological clarity does not necessitate unfiltered clarity in every text and every word. As Mark Thompson has summarized, "Some individual texts will be difficult. We have no promise that we will have *all* the answers."[71]

Rather, God has delivered a body of diverse yet organically cohesive revelation, the canon of Holy Scripture, which discloses his grand purposes unambiguously. Just as light refracts through the points of a brilliant cut diamond, the diverse words of revelation luminously display distinct features of the single jewel of redemption. Perspicuity comes from words, as these sundry words in their diverse genres complement one another in divinely tooled brilliance. Thus, perspicuity refers to Scripture's embedded, canonical, self-interpreting meaning. To affirm clarity in terms of organic meaning does not detach clarity from the words of Scripture, because it is God's condescending communication *in the words* that conveys his perspicuous message. We cannot extract clarity from verbal inspira-

---

71. Thompson, *Clear and Present Word*, 162. He continues pointedly, "On some issues there will be room for the legitimate exercise of Christian freedom. Yet our confidence in the goodness of God and his capacity to make his mind known to us without distortion should generate an expectation that the basic contours of a Christian response to even the most recent developments in thought and practice can be found in the Scriptures."

tion any more than we can remove a point of refracted light from a gem. The divinely inspired words function in their multi-faceted and mutually explanatory forms to communicate singularly and perspicuously the redemptive plan of God in Christ. Through the ages, God has spoken about his redemptive work in his Son, and he has spoken unambiguously. That is absolutely clear.

## CONCLUSION

In resistance to God's eternal simplicity, his redemptive intention, and his verbal clarity, attempts to squelch his voice persist. Some brashly reject Scripture's authority; others employ reader-corrupted ingenuity and impertinently place confidence outside of God's inscripturated Word. Thinking themselves free and clear, today's readers darken biblical perspicuity through self-generated hermeneutical models. So, they contend, Scripture is not clear, but the autonomous freedom to interpret it surely is.

With roots in history's first sin, such human-centered methods present nothing new. On the heels of the command and covenantal warning in Genesis 2 comes the tyrannical fall in Genesis 3. Tempting our first parents ("you" is plural in Gen. 3:1–5), Satan sabotages divine revelation: "Now the serpent was more crafty than any other beast of the field that the Lord God had made. He said to the woman, 'Did God actually say, "You shall not eat of any tree in the garden?"'" (Gen. 3:1). In this conniving ploy, God's enemy injects doubt about the Creator by questioning the authoritative clarity of his Word. *Did he really say? Did he really mean?* The wily rhetoric persuaded Adam and Eve to implement a new self-reliant hermeneutic in which they pitted their created intellects against their Creator's clear commands. Thus, long before Fish came the Garden serpent, whose lies poisoned the minds of our first parents, and inaugurated the age of human-sourced hermeneutics.

Since this Edenic ruse, the weeds of unbelief have never shriveled; their roots have sought and found new hearts to penetrate in every generation, and now in the twenty-first century, these weeds of unbelief have found yet more fertile soil. Whether it is the scholarly community in false humility pronouncing the perspicuous Word a murky mess, or the postmodern communities of faith that consciously or unconsciously adopt Fish-friendly paradigms for interpretation, the clarity of God's Word as God's Word suffers a rebellious eclipse. Ancient serpentine doubts endure: *Is God's Word reliable? Should I place my trust in it?* As Lorraine Boettner reminds us, "Ultimately every person has to make a choice between the *vox Dei* and the *vox mundi,* the voice of God and the voice of the world."[72] One posture characterizes redemptive understanding, and the other exposes a darkened heart.

Under the blinding pressure of scholarly and cultural unbelief, it might appear that all certainty is lost, that we are left in the morass of corrupted communication and of an obscure, inaccessible word. Not so. In the revealed Jesus Christ, the Protagonist of Scripture, we find gracious, intentional, personal perspicuity; the divine voice of Scripture pierces through the unbelieving murk with eloquent and immanent clarity. Scripture is that personal Word from the God of heaven revealing his personal Son, who himself is the *Word,* and who illumines us by his personal Holy Spirit to grasp clearly what he has said. "Finally, there is a word that meets our deepest and most desperate need, our need to be clean from our sin and all its debilitating consequences, a word with power to cleanse, with a detergency strong enough to restore the image we bear to its full luster, and so, to strip away the impurities that pollute our communication at every level and in every form."[73] By divine and gracious purpose, perspicuity simply cannot go away, and man can no more snuff it out than he can snuff out the Son of God himself.

Without question, the hyper-hermeneutical age with its reader-centered views of meaning energizes the current clarity crisis.

72. Loraine Boettner, *Studies in Theology* (Philadelphia: Presbyterian and Reformed, 1965), 47.
73. Gaffin, "Speech and the Image of God," 188.

This dark cloud prevails not only because perspicuity is denied or marginalized, but because perspicuity has itself been recast as a human product rather than a biblical property. The very protest against perspicuity commonly garbles the divine gift, confusing the nature of God's Word with the interpretation of it, and conflating biblical perspicuity and biblical illumination. Neither the Author nor Communicator of confusion, God cannot breathe out fog. His inscripturated Word is clear because he is the Speaker. Infinitely competent and redemptively purposeful, almighty God has acted *in history* and interpreted those acts for us verbally *in history*. His progressively revealed words climactically converge in his Son, in whom the clarity of his divine redemptive purpose shines gloriously and consummately (John 1:14; Heb. 1:3). Biblical revelation then leads us unswervingly to Jesus Christ, and to understand his revelation properly necessitates the Spirit-given clarity of the text and its concomitant, the Spirit-wrought understanding in the reader. According to God's gracious will, both perspicuity and illumination are gifts: the first a characteristic of the revealed Word and the second a change in the redeemed reader. Perspicuity remains an inviolable characteristic of this divine verbal revelation, present because of who God is and how he has purposed to reveal himself. Illumination remains a necessary work of spiritual transformation by the Spirit of God in the reader, accomplished because of who God is and how he has purposed to reveal himself.

Biblical perspicuity ensures interpretive perspicacity. God has spoken clearly in his Word and he intends his people to understand. He cannot and will not be denied.

# Bibliography

Aichele, George. "Canon, Ideology, and the Emergence of an Imperial Church." In *Canon and Canonicity: The Formation and Use of Scripture*, edited by Einar Thomassen, 45–65. Copenhagen: Museum Tusculanum Press, 2010.

Aland, Kurt. *The Problem of the New Testament Canon*. London: A. R. Mowbray & Co., 1962.

Alexander, Loveday. *The Preface to Luke's Gospel*. Cambridge: Cambridge University Press, 1993.

Allert, Craig D. *A High View of Scripture? The Authority of the Bible and the Formation of the New Testament Canon*. Grand Rapids: Baker Academic, 2007.

Augustine, *Contra Faustum*. A Select Library of the Nicene and Post-Nicene Fathers of the Christian Church 1. Grand Rapids: Eerdmans, 1989.

Aune, David E. "Luke 1:1–4: Historical or Scientific *Prooimion*?" In *Paul, Luke and the Graeco-Roman World: Essays in Honour of Alexander J. M. Wedderburn*, edited by Alf Christophersen et al., 138–48. Sheffield, UK: Sheffield Academic Press, 2002.

Barr, James. *The Scope and Authority of the Bible*. Philadelphia, Westminster, 1980.

———. *Holy Scripture: Canon, Authority and Criticism*. Philadelphia: Westminster, 1983.

Barrerra, J. C. T. "Origins of a Tripartite Old Testament Canon." In *The Canon Debate*, edited by Lee Martin McDonald and James A. Sanders, 128–45. Peabody, MA: Hendrickson, 2002.

Barth, Karl. *Church Dogmatics*. Vol. 1, translated by G. W. Bromiley and T. F. Torrance. Edinburgh: T&T Clark, 1975.

Barton, John. "Canonical Approaches Ancient and Modern." In *The Biblical Canons*, edited by J.-M. Auwers and H. J. de Jonge, 199–209. Leuven, Belg.: Leuven University Press, 2003.

———. *The Spirit and the Letter: Studies in the Biblical Canon*. London: SPCK, 1997.

Bauer, Walter. *Rechtgläubigkeit und Ketzerei im ältesten Christentum*. Tübingen: J. C. B. Mohr, 1934.

Bavinck, Herman. *Reformed Dogmatics*. Edited by John Bolt. Translated by John Vriend. 4 vols. Grand Rapids: Baker, 1992–2008.

Beckwith, Roger T. *The Old Testament Canon of the New Testament Church and Its Background in Early Judaism*. Grand Rapids: Eerdmans, 1986.

Berger, Peter. "Epistemological Modesty: An Interview with Peter Berger." *Christian Century*, October 29, 1997, 972–78.

Berkouwer, G. C. *General Revelation*. Grand Rapids: Eerdmans, 1955.

———. *Holy Scripture*. Grand Rapids: Eerdmans, 1975.

Boettner, Loraine. *Studies in Theology*. Philadelphia: Presbyterian and Reformed, 1965.

Brooks, David. "The Big Test." *New York Times*, February 23, 2009.

Brown, Dan. *The Da Vinci Code*. New York: Doubleday, 2003.

Brown, Jeannine K. *Scripture as Communication: Introducing Biblical Hermeneutics*. Grand Rapids: Baker, 2007.

Brown, Schuyler. "The Role of the Prologues in Determining the Purpose of Luke-Acts." In *Perspectives on Luke-Acts*, edited by Charles H. Talbert, 99–111. Edinburgh: T&T Clark, 1978.

Buchanan, James. *The Doctrine of Justification: An Outline of Its History in the Church and Its Exposition from Scripture*. Edinburgh: T&T Clark, 1867.

Buck, C. "The Early Order of the Pauline Corpus." *JBL* 68 (1949): 351–57.

Calhoun, David B. *Princeton Seminary*. 2 vols. Edinburgh: Banner of Truth, 1996.

Callahan, James. *The Clarity of Scripture: History, Theology, and Contemporary Literary Studies*. Downers Grove, IL: InterVarsity Press, 2001.

Calvin, John. *Institutes of the Christian Religion*. Edited by John T. McNeill. Translated by Ford Lewis Battles. 2 vols. Philadelphia: Westminster, 1975.

———. *Tracts and Treatises*. Translated by Henry Beveridge. Grand Rapids: Eerdmans, 1958.

Campenhausen, Hans von. *The Formation of the Christian Bible*. London: Adam and Charles Black, 1972.

Cannata, Raymond D. "Warfield and the Doctrine of Scripture." In *B. B. Warfield: Essays on His Life and Thought*, edited by Gary L. W. Johnson, 92–107. Phillipsburg, NJ: P&R Publishing, 2007.

Carroll, K. L. "The Expansion of the Pauline Corpus." *JBL* 72 (1953): 230–37.

Carson, D. A. *The Gagging of God: Christianity Confronts Pluralism*. Grand Rapids: Zondervan, 1996.

Chapman, Stephen B. "How the Biblical Canon Began: Working Models and Open Questions." In *Homer, the Bible, and Beyond: Literary and Religious Canons in the Ancient World*, edited by Margalit Finkelberg and Guy G. Strousma, 29–51. Leiden: Brill, 2003.

———. *The Law and the Prophets: A Study in the Old Testament Canon Formation*. Tübingen: Mohr Siebeck, 2000.

Childs, Brevard S. "The One Gospel in Four Witnesses." In *The Rule of Faith: Scripture, Canon, and Creed in a Critical Age*, edited by Ephraim Radner and George Sumner, 51–62. Harrisburg, PA: Morehouse, 1998.

Collins, C. John. *Did Adam and Eve Really Exist? Who They Were and Why You Should Care*. Wheaton, IL: Crossway, 2011.

Cullmann, Oscar. "The Tradition." In *The Early Church*, 59–99. London: SCM Press, 1956.

Dempster, Stephen G. "Canons on the Right and Canons on the Left: Finding a Resolution in the Canon Debate." *JETS* 52 (2009): 47–77.

Dungan, David L. *Constantine's Bible: Politics and the Making of the New Testament*. Philadelphia: Fortress Press, 2006.

Dunn, J. D. G. *Unity and Diversity in the New Testament: An Inquiry into the Character of Early Christianity*. London: SCM Press, 1990.

Ehrman, Bart D. *Forged: Writing in the Name of God—Why the Bible's Authors Are Not Who We Think They Are*. New York: HarperOne, 2011.

———. *Jesus, Interrupted: Revealing the Hidden Contradictions in the Bible (and Why We Don't Know about Them)*. San Francisco: HarperOne, 2009.

———. *Lost Christianities: The Battles for Scripture and the Faiths We Never Knew*. New York: Oxford University Press, 2002.

———. *Misquoting Jesus: The Story behind Who Changed the Bible and Why*. San Francisco: HarperCollins, 2005.

Enns, Peter. *Inspiration and Incarnation*. Grand Rapids: Baker Academic, 2005.

*Evangelical Convictions: A Theological Exposition of the Statement of Faith of the Evangelical Free Church of America*. Minneapolis: Free Church Publications, 2011.

Fee, Gordon D. *The First Epistle to the Corinthians*. New International Commentary on the New Testament. Grand Rapids: Eerdmans, 1987.

Ferguson, Everett. "The Covenant Idea in the Second Century." In *Texts and Testaments: Critical Essays on the Bible and the Early Church Fathers*, edited by W. Eugene March, 135–62. San Antonio: Trinity University Press, 1980.

———. Review of *The Muratorian Fragment and the Development of the Canon*, by Geoffrey Mark Hahneman. *JTS* 44 (1993): 691–97.

Ferguson, Sinclair. "How Does the Bible Look at Itself?" In *Inerrancy and Hermeneutic*, edited by Harvie Conn, 47–66. Grand Rapids: Baker, 1988.

Fish, Stanley. *Is There a Text in This Class? The Authority of Interpretive Communities*. Cambridge, MA: Harvard University Press, 1980.

Frame, John M. *The Doctrine of the Knowledge of God*. Phillipsburg, NJ: Presbyterian and Reformed, 1985.

———. *The Doctrine of the Word of God*. Phillipsburg, NJ: P&R Publishing, 2010.

Franke, John. *The Character of Theology: An Introduction to Its Nature, Task, and Purpose*. Grand Rapids: Baker Academic, 2005.

———. "Reforming Theology: Toward a Postmodern Reformed Dogmatics." *WTJ* 65 (Spring 2003): 1–26.

Funk, Robert W. *The Five Gospels: What Did Jesus Really Say?* New York: Polebridge, 1993.

Gaffin, Richard B. "Speech and the Image of God: Biblical Reflections on Language and Its Uses." In *The Pattern of Sound Doctrine: Systematic Theology at the Westminster Seminaries: Essays in Honor of Robert B. Strimple*, edited by David Van Drunen. Phillipsburg, NJ: P&R Publishing, 2004.

Gamble, Harry Y. *The New Testament Canon: Its Making and Meaning.* Philadelphia: Fortress Press, 1985.

———. "The Redaction of the Pauline Letters and the Formation of the Pauline Corpus." *JBL* 94 (1975): 403–18.

Gerstner, John H. "Warfield's Case for Biblical Inerrancy." In *God's Inerrant Word*, edited by John W. Montgomery, 116–20. Newburgh, IN: Trinity Press, 1974.

Grant, Robert. *The Formation of the New Testament.* New York: Harper & Row, 1965.

Grudem, Wayne. "The Perspicuity of Scripture." *Themelios* 34, 3 (2009): 288–308.

———. "'A Redemptive-Movement Hermeneutic: The Slavery Analogy' (Ch 22) and 'Gender Equality and Homosexuality' (Ch 23) by William J. Webb." *JBMW* 10, 1 (Spring 2005): 96–120.

Hahneman, Geoffrey M. *The Muratorian Fragment and the Development of the Canon.* Oxford: Clarendon, 1992.

Hanson, Kenneth. *Secrets from the Lost Bible: Hidden Scriptures Found.* Vancouver: Council Oak Books, 2004.

Harnack, Adolf von. *History of Dogma.* 3rd ed. Translated by Neil Buchanan. 7 vols. 1894–1899. Reprint, New York: Dover, 1961.

Harrington, Daniel J. "The Reception of Walter Bauer's *Orthodoxy and Heresy in Earliest Christianity* during the Last Decade." *HTR* 77 (1980): 289–98.

Hauerwas, Stanley. *Unleashing the Scriptures: Freeing the Bible from Captivity to America.* Nashville: Abingdon Press, 1993.

Heckel, T. K. *Vom Evangelium des Markus zum viergestaltigen Evangelium.* Tübingen: J. C. B. Mohr, 1999.

Helm, Paul. *The Divine Revelation: The Basic Issues.* London: Marshall, Morgan & Scott, 1982.

Helm, Paul, and Carl Trueman, eds. *The Trustworthiness of God: Perspectives on the Nature of Scripture.* Grand Rapids: Eerdmans, 2002.

Helseth, Paul Kjoss. *"Right Reason" and the Princeton Mind: An Unorthodox Proposal*. Phillipsburg, NJ: P&R Publishing, 2010.

Hempton, David. *Evangelical Disenchantment: Nine Portraits of Faith and Doubt*. New Haven, CT: Yale University Press, 2008.

Henne, P. "La Datation du canon de Muratori." *RB* 100 (1993): 54–75.

Heppe, Heinrich. *Reformed Dogmatics*. Translated by G. T. Thomson. London: George Allen and Unwin, Ltd., 1950.

Hill, Charles E. "The Debate over the Muratorian Fragment and the Development of the Canon." *WTJ* 57 (1995): 437–52.

———. "The New Testament Canon: Deconstructio Ad Absurdum?" *JETS* 52 (2009): 101–19.

———. *Who Chose the Gospels? Probing the Great Gospel Conspiracy*. Oxford: Oxford University Press, 2010.

Hillers, Delbert R. *Covenant: The History of a Biblical Idea*. Baltimore: Johns Hopkins University Press, 1969.

Hodge, Charles. *Systematic Theology*. 3 vols. Peabody, MA: Hendrickson, 1999.

Hoffecker, Andrew W. *Piety and the Princeton Theologians: Archibald Alexander, Charles Hodge, and Benjamin Warfield*. Phillipsburg, NJ: Presbyterian and Reformed, 1981.

Hoffmann, R. Joseph. *Marcion: On the Restitution of Christianity: An Essay on the Development of Radical Paulinist Theology in the Second Century*. Chico, CA: Scholars Press, 1984.

Horton, Michael S. *People and Place: A Covenant Ecclesiology*. Louisville: Westminster John Knox, 2008.

Hurtado, Larry W. *The Earliest Christian Artifacts: Manuscripts and Christian Origins*. Grand Rapids: Eerdmans, 2006.

Jenkins, Philip. *The New Faces of Christianity: Believing the Bible in the Global South*. New York: Oxford University Press, 2006.

Jensen, Peter. *The Revelation of God*. Downers Grove, IL: InterVarsity Press, 2002.

Keener, Craig. *The Historical Jesus of the Gospels*. Grand Rapids: Eerdmans, 2009.

Kelly, J. N. D. *A Commentary on the Pastoral Epistles*. Peabody, MA: Hendrickson, 1960.

Kelsey, David H. *The Uses of Scripture in Recent Theology*. Philadelphia, Fortress Press, 1975.

Kinzig, W. "καινή διαθήκη: The Title of the New Testament in the Second and Third Centuries." *JTS* 45 (1994): 519–44.

Kline, Meredith G. *The Structure of Biblical Authority*. Eugene, OR: Wipf and Stock, 1997.

Koester, Helmut. *Ancient Christian Gospels: Their History and Development*. London: SCM Press, 1990.

———. "Apocryphal and Canonical Gospels." *HTR* 73 (1980): 105–30.

Köstenberger, Andreas J., and Michael J. Kruger. *The Heresy of Orthodoxy: How Contemporary Culture's Fascination with Diversity Has Reshaped Our Understanding of Early Christianity*. Wheaton, IL: Crossway, 2010.

Krosney, Herbert. *The Lost Gospel: The Quest for the Gospel of Judas Iscariot*. Hanover, PA: National Geographic Society, 2006.

Kruger, Michael J. *Canon Revisited: Establishing the Origins and Authority of the New Testament Books*. Wheaton, IL: Crossway, 2012.

Küng, Hans. *Infallible? An Enquiry*. London: Collins, 1972.

Lane, A.N. S. "B. B. Warfield on the Humanity of Scripture." *VE* 16 (1986): 77–94.

Letham, Robert. *The Holy Trinity: In Scripture, History, Theology, and Worship*. Phillipsburg, NJ: P&R Publishing, 2004.

Lightfoot, John. *The Harmony, Chronicle, and Order of the New Testament*. Vol. 3 of *The Whole Works of the Reverend and Learned John Lightfoot*, edited by John Rogers Pitman. London: J. F. Dove, 1822.

Luther, Martin. *The Bondage of the Will: A New Translation of De Servo Arbitrio (1525), Martin Luther's Reply to Erasmus of Rotterdam*. Translated by J. I. Packer and O. R. Johnston. Westwood, NJ: Fleming H. Revell, 1957.

Machen, J. Gresham. *Christianity and Liberalism*. 1923. Reprint, Grand Rapids: Eerdmans, 2009.

Macleod, Donald. *A Faith to Live By: Understanding Christian Doctrines*. Fearn, Ross-shire, UK: Christian Focus, 1998.

Marshall, I. Howard. "Orthodoxy and Heresy in Earlier Christianity." *Themelios* 2 (1976): 5–14.

McCue, James. "Orthodoxy and Heresy: Walter Bauer and the Valentinians." *VC* 33 (1979): 118–30.

McDonald, Lee Martin. *The Biblical Canon: Its Origin, Transmission, and Authority.* Peabody, MA: Hendrickson, 2007.

———. *Forgotten Scriptures: The Selection and Rejection of Early Religious Writings.* Louisville: Westminster John Knox, 2009.

———. *The Formation of the Christian Biblical Canon.* Peabody, MA: Hendrickson, 1995.

McGowan, A. T. B. *The Divine Authenticity of Scripture: Retrieving an Evangelical Heritage.* Downers Grove, IL: InterVarsity Press, 2007.

McLaren, Brian D. *Generous Orthodoxy.* El Cajon, CA: Youth Specialties, 2004.

Meier, John P. "The Inspiration of Scripture: But What Counts as Scripture?" *Mid-Stream* 38 (1999): 71–78.

Mendenhall, G. E. "Covenant Forms in Israelite Tradition." *BA* 17 (1954): 50–76.

Metzger, Bruce, and Bart Ehrman. *The Text of the New Testament.* 4th ed. New York: Oxford University Press, 2005.

Muller, Richard A. *Holy Scripture: The Cognitive Foundation of Theology.* Vol. 2 of *Post-Reformation Reformed Dogmatics: The Rise and Development of Reformed Orthodoxy, ca. 1520 to ca. 1725.* Grand Rapids: Baker Academic, 2003.

———. *Prolegomena to Theology.* Vol. 1 of *Post-Reformation Reformed Dogmatics: The Rise and Development of Reformed Orthodoxy, ca. 1520 to ca. 1725.* Grand Rapids: Baker, 1987.

Murray, John. "The Attestation of Scripture." In *The Infallible Word: A Symposium by the Members of the Faculty of Westminster Theological Seminary,* edited by N. B. Stonehouse and Paul Woolley, 1–54. Philadelphia: Presbyterian and Reformed, 1946.

Newbigin, Lesslie. *Proper Confidence: Faith, Doubt and Certainty in Christian Discipleship.* Grand Rapids: Eerdmans, 1995.

Noll, Mark. *The New Shape of World Christianity: How American Experience Reflects Global Faith.* Downers Grove, IL: IVP Academic, 2009.

Noll, Mark, and Carolyn Nystrom. *Clouds of Witnesses: Christian Voices from Africa and Asia.* Downers Grove, IL: InterVarsity Press, 2011.

Packer, J. I. *Fundamentalism and the Word of God*. Grand Rapids: Eerdmans, 1992.

———. *God Has Spoken: Revelation and the Bible*. Downers Grove, IL: InterVarsity Press, 1979.

———. *God Speaks to Man: Revelation and the Bible*. Christian Foundations 6. Philadelphia: Westminster, 1965.

Pagels, Elaine. *Beyond Belief: The Secret Gospel of Thomas*. New York: Random House, 2003.

Petersen, W. L. "The Diatessaron and the Fourfold Gospel." In *The Earliest Gospels*, ed. Charles Horton, 50–68. London: T&T Clark International, 2004.

Peterson, David. "God and Scripture in Hebrews." In *The Trustworthiness of God: Perspectives on the Nature of Scripture*, edited by Paul Helm and Carl Trueman, 118–38. Grand Rapids: Eerdmans, 2002.

Piper, John, and D. A. Carson. *The Pastor as Scholar and the Scholar as Pastor*. Wheaton, IL: Crossway, 2011.

Plessis-Mornay, Philippe du. *A Worke Concerning the Trunesse of Christian Religion, Written in French: Against Atheists, Epicures, Paynims, Iewes, Mahumetists, and Other Infidels*. Translated by Sir Philip Sidney Knight and Arthur Golding. London: George Eld, 1604.

Poirier, J. C. "Scripture and Canon." In *The Sacred Text*, edited by Michael Bird and Michael Pahl, 83–98. Piscataway, NJ: Gorgias Press, 2010.

Porter, Stanley E. "When and How Was the Pauline Canon Compiled? An Assessment of Theories." In *The Pauline Canon*, edited by Stanley E. Porter, 95–127. Leiden: Brill, 2004.

Poythress, Vern S. *In the Beginning Was the Word: Language—A God-Centered Approach*. Wheaton, IL: Crossway, 2009.

Provan, Iain. "Canons to the Left of Him: Brevard Childs, His Critics, and the Future of Old Testament Theology." *SJT* 50 (1997): 1–38.

Rhoads, John H. "Josephus Misdated the Census of Quirinius." *JETS* 54, 1 (March 2011): 65–87.

Ridderbos, Herman. "The Canon of the New Testament." In *Revelation and the Bible: Contemporary Evangelical Thought*, edited by Carl F. H. Henry, 187–201. Grand Rapids: Baker, 1958.

———. *Redemptive History and the New Testament Scriptures*. Translated by H. de Jongste. Revised by Richard B. Gaffin Jr. Phillipsburg, NJ: Presbyterian and Reformed, 1988.

Robbins, Vernon K. "The Claims of the Prologues and Greco-Roman Rhetoric: The Prefaces to Luke and Acts in Light of Greco-Roman Rhetorical Strategies." In *Jesus and the Heritage of Israel*, edited by David P. Moessner, 63–83. Harrisburg, PA: Trinity Press International, 1999.

Robinson, James M. *The Secrets of Judas: The Story of the Misunderstood Disciple and His Lost Gospel*. San Francisco: HarperSanFrancisco, 2006.

Robinson, James M., and Helmut Koester. *Trajectories through Early Christianity*. Philadelphia: Fortress Press, 1971.

Robinson, Thomas. *The Bauer Thesis Examined: The Geography of Heresy in the Early Christian Church*. Lewiston, NY: Edwin Mellen, 1989.

Rogers, Jack, and Donald McKim. *The Authority and Interpretation of the Bible*. San Francisco: Harper & Row, 1979.

Sandeen, Ernest R. *The Origins of Fundamentalism: Toward a Historical Interpretation*. Philadelphia: Fortress Press, 1968.

———. *The Roots of Fundamentalism: British and American Millenarianism, 1800–1930*. Chicago: University of Chicago Press, 1970.

Sanneh, Lamin. *Whose Religion Is Christianity? The Gospel beyond the West*. Grand Rapids: Eerdmans, 2003.

Schwöbel, C. "The Creature of the Word: Recovering the Ecclesiology of the Reformers." In *On Being the Church: Essays on the Christian Community*, edited by Colin E. Gunton and Daniel W. Hardy, 110–55. Edinburgh: T&T Clark, 1989.

Sexton, Jason. "How Far beyond Chicago? Assessing Recent Attempts to Reframe the Inerrancy Debate." *Themelios* 34, 1 (2009): 26–49.

Shanks, Hershel. "Losing Faith: Who Did and Who Didn't. How Scholarship Affects Scholars." *BAR* 33, 2 (March–April 2007): 50–57.

Silva, Moisés. *Has the Church Misread the Bible? The History of Interpretation in the Light of Current Issues*. Foundations of Contemporary Interpretation. Grand Rapids: Zondervan, 1996.

———. "Old Princeton, Westminster, and Inerrancy." In *B. B. Warfield: Essays on His Life and Thought*, edited by Gary L. W. Johnson, 76–91. Phillipsburg, NJ: P&R Publishing, 2007.

Smith, Christian. *The Bible Made Impossible: Why Biblicism Is Not a Truly Evangelical Reading of Scripture*. Grand Rapids: Brazos Press, 2011.

———. *How to Go from a Good Evangelical to a Committed Catholic in Ninety-five Difficult Steps*. Eugene, OR: Wipf and Stock, 2011.

Smith, D. Moody. "When Did the Gospels Become Scripture?" *JBL* 119 (2000): 3–20.

Smith, James K. A. *The Fall of Interpretation: Philosophical Foundations for a Creational Hermeneutic*. Downers Grove, IL: InterVarsity Press, 2000.

Sparks, Kenton L. *God's Word in Human Words: An Evangelical Appropriation of Critical Biblical Scholarship*. Grand Rapids: Baker, 2008.

Steinmann, Andrew E. *The Oracles of God: The Old Testament Canon*. St. Louis: Concordia Academic Press, 1999.

Sundberg, Albert C. "Canon Muratori: A Fourth-Century List." *HTR* 66 (1973): 1–41.

———. "Towards a Revised History of the New Testament Canon." *SE* 4 (1968): 452–61.

Thiselton, Anthony. "Authority and Hermeneutics: Some Proposals for a More Creative Agenda." In *A Pathway into the Holy Scripture*, edited by Philip Satterthwaite and David F. Wright, 110–15. Grand Rapids: Eerdmans, 1994.

Thompson, Alan. "Pietist Critique of Inerrancy? J. A. Bengel's *Gnomon* as a Test Case." *JETS* 47 (2004): 71–88.

Thompson, Mark D. *Clear and Present Word: The Clarity of Scripture*. New Testament Studies in Biblical Theology 21. Downers Grove, IL: InterVarsity Press, 2006.

Trobisch, David. *Die Entstehung der Paulusbriefsammlung: Studien zu den Anfängen christlicher Publizistik (Novum testamentum et orbis antiquus)*. Göttingen: Vandenhoeck & Ruprecht, 1989.

Turner, H. E. W. *The Pattern of Christian Truth: A Study in the Relations between Orthodoxy and Heresy in the Early Church*. London: A. R. Mowbray, 1954.

Turretin, Francis. *Institutes of Elenctic Theology*. Edited by James T. Dennison. Translated by George Musgrave Giger. 3 vols. Phillipsburg, NJ: P&R Publishing, 1992.

Ulrich, Eugene. "The Notion and Definition of Canon." In *The Canon Debate*, edited by Lee Martin McDonald and James A. Sanders, 21–35. Peabody, MA: Hendrickson, 2002.

Unnik, W. C. van. "ἡ καινή διαθήκη—A Problem in the Early History of the Canon." *StP* 4 (1961): 212–27.

Vander Stelt, John. *Philosophy and Scripture: A Study of Old Princeton and Westminster Theology*. Marlburg, NJ: Mack Publishing, 1978.

Vanhoozer, Kevin. "God's Mighty Speech-Acts: The Doctrine of Scripture Today." In *A Pathway into the Holy Scripture*, edited by Philip Satterthwaite and David F. Wright, 143–81. Grand Rapids: Eerdmans, 1994.

———. *Is There a Meaning in This Text? The Bible, the Reader, and the Morality of Literary Knowledge*. Grand Rapids: Zondervan, 1998.

Van Til, Cornelius. "Nature and Scripture." In *The Infallible Word: A Symposium by the Members of the Faculty of Westminster Theological Seminary*, edited by N. B. Stonehouse and Paul Woolley, 263–301. 2nd ed. Philadelphia: Presbyterian and Reformed, 1967.

Verheyden, J. "The Canon Muratori: A Matter of Dispute." In *The Biblical Canons*, edited by J.-M. Auwers and H. J. de Jonge, 487–556. Leuven, Belg.: Leuven University Press, 2003.

Vos, Geerhardus. *Biblical Theology*. Edinburgh: Banner of Truth, 1975.

———. "The Idea of Biblical Theology as a Science and as a Theological Discipline." In *Redemptive History and Biblical Interpretation: The Shorter Writings of Geerhardus Vos*, edited by Richard B. Gaffin Jr., 3–24. Phillipsburg, NJ: Presbyterian and Reformed, 1980.

Walton, John H. *The Lost World of Genesis One: Ancient Cosmology and the Origins Debate*. Downers Grove, IL: InterVarsity Press, 2009.

Ward, Timothy. *Words of Life: Scripture as the Living and Active Word of God*. Downers Grove, IL: InverVarsity Press, 2009.

Warfield, Benjamin B. *Benjamin B. Warfield: Selected Shorter Writings*. Edited by John E. Meeter. 4th ed. 2 vols. Phillipsburg, NJ: P&R Publishing, 2001.

———. *Calvin and Augustine*. Edited by Samuel G. Craig. Philadelphia: Presbyterian and Reformed, 1956.

———. *The Inspiration and Authority of the Bible*. Edited by Samuel G. Craig. Philadelphia: Presbyterian and Reformed, 1948.

———. *The Westminster Assembly and Its Work*. New York: Oxford University Press, 1931.

Webb, William J. *Slaves, Women, and Homosexuals: Exploring the Hermeneutics of Cultural Analysis*. Downers Grove, IL: IVP Academic, 2001.

Webster, John. "'A Great and Meritorious Act of the Church'? The Dogmatic Location of the Canon." In *Die Einheit der Schrift und die Vielfalt des Kanons*, edited by John Barton and Michael Wolter, 95–126. Berlin: Walter de Gruyter, 2003.

———. *Holy Scripture: A Dogmatic Sketch*. Cambridge: Cambridge University Press, 2003.

———. "The Self-Organizing Power of the Gospel of Christ: Episcopacy and Community Formation." In *Word and Church: Essays in Church Dogmatics*, 191–210. Edinburgh: T&T Clark, 2001.

Woodbridge, John. *Biblical Authority: A Critique of the Rogers/McKim Proposal*. Grand Rapids: Zondervan, 1982.

———. "Evangelical Self-Identity and the Doctrine of Biblical Inerrancy." In *Understanding the Times: New Testament Studies in the 21st Century: Essays in Honor of D. A. Carson on the Occasion of His 65th Birthday*, edited by Andreas Köstenberger and Robert W. Yarbrough, 104–38. Wheaton, IL: Crossway, 2011.

Woodbridge, John D., and Randal H. Balmer. "The Princetonians and Biblical Authority: An Assessment of the Ernest Sandeen Proposal." In *Scripture and Truth*, edited by D. A. Carson and John D. Woodbridge, 254–69. Grand Rapids: Baker, 1983.

Woodbridge, John, and D. A. Carson, eds. *Hermeneutics, Authority, and Canon*. Eugene, OR: Wipf and Stock, 2005.

———. *Scripture and Truth*. Grand Rapids: Baker, 1992.

Wright, N. T. "How Can the Bible Be Authoritative?" *VE* 21 (1991): 7–32.

———. *The Last Word: Scripture and the Authority of God*. San Francisco: HarperSanFrancisco, 2005.

———. *The Resurrection of the Son of God.* Vol. 3 of *Christian Origins and the Question of God.* Minneapolis: Fortress Press, 2003.

———. *Simply Christian: Why Christianity Makes Sense.* San Francisco: HarperSanFrancisco, 2006.

Yarbrough, Robert W. "Godet, Frédéric Louis." In *Dictionary of Major Biblical Interpreters*, edited by Donald K. McKim, 465–69. Downers Grove, IL: IVP Academic, 2007.

# Index of Subjects and Names

# Contributors

John M. Frame is the J. D. Trimble Professor of Systematic Theology and Philosophy at Reformed Theological Seminary in Orlando, Florida.

David B. Garner is associate professor of systematic theology at Westminster Theological Seminary in Philadelphia, Pennsylvania.

Michael J. Kruger is professor of New Testament at Reformed Theological Seminary in Charlotte, North Carolina.

K. Scott Oliphint is professor of apologetics and systematic theology at Westminster Theological Seminary in Philadelphia, Pennsylvania.

Vern S. Poythress is professor of New Testament interpretation at Westminster Theological Seminary in Philadelphia, Pennsylvania.

Michael D. Williams is professor of systematic theology at Covenant Theological Seminary in St. Louis, Missouri.

Robert W. Yarbrough is professor of New Testament at Covenant Theological Seminary in St. Louis, Missouri.